The College President

The College President

RALPH PRATOR

President
San Fernando Valley State College

1963

The Center for Applied Research in Education, Inc.
Washington, D.C.

Library of Congress
Catalog Card No.: 62-18291

PRINTED IN THE UNITED STATES OF AMERICA
14803

Foreword

The college presidency as it has developed in the United States is unique in the history of higher education. Almost from its beginning in this country, the office has carried more power than a comparable position carries anywhere else in the world. Many students of higher education have found this centering of power in a person a strange phenomenon in a country that is jealous of its democracy.

Over the more than three hundred years during which our colleges and universities have been developing on this continent, faculties have often galled under the power of willful presidents. Equally often, faculties have been inspired to work and sacrifice because of the leadership of great presidents who have used their positions wisely, and institutions have risen to new levels of effectiveness. Many keen observers have felt that the college president because of the special nature of his office is subject to an occupational disease: a special kind of self-centeredness that results from too long being a symbol of authority in a type of community that should respect only truth as authority.

All depends upon how the president wears his position; and perhaps it is difficult or impossible to predict what an office will do to a man or what he will do with an office before he takes it on. On this point the poet Sophocles wisely said:

> But hard it is to learn
> The mind of any mortal or the heart,
> Till he be tried in chief authority.
> Power shows the man.

Fortunately, this important office is being given increasingly careful study by those interested in higher education. Many college and university presidents have written about their experiences. As a rule, these accounts have been in the nature of reminiscences and have not been designed as analyses of the office and its relation to the special processes of higher education. Dr. Ralph Prator's monograph *The College President* is a serious attempt at such an analysis by a man presently engaged in the work of the presidency. Hence the volume is an important contribution to the growing literature in higher education.

How does a person enmeshed in the responsibilities of the college presidency conceive the role of the president? What does he think of academic freedom and the responsibility of the faculty? Of his relation to students? Of his leadership opportunities? Of the nature of higher education? Of the popularization of higher learning? These and many other questions arise in the mind of the student of higher education—faculty member, fellow president, board member, citizen—as he opens this book.

The reader is rewarded, for Dr. Prator is an able and sincere student of the problems of colleges and universities, and his study and thought have been seasoned by extended experience. Thus the book has a quality of freshness and genuineness which a volume based merely upon research does not have. Reading the book is very much like talking with a thoughtful man who is now wrestling with the problems about which he writes. Anyone who desires a better understanding of higher education will find interest and profit in sharing this man's study, thought, and experience.

E. V. PULLIAS
Professor of Higher Education
University of Southern California

Contents

CHAPTER I

Introduction   1

Historical Background   1
The Literature   17

CHAPTER II

Nature of the Office   20

Traditions of the Office   20
The College President as Others See Him   23
*The President as Interpreter and Defender of
    Aims*   27
The President and the Board of Control   29
The Duties of the Office   37

CHAPTER III

Leadership in Decision Making   53

Working with Administrative Faculty   53
Working with the Trustees   58
*Working with the Teaching Faculty and Faculty
    Organizations*   62

CONTENTS

CHAPTER IV

The Continuum   75

Alma Mater   75
Presidential Vision and Imagination   76
Expectations of the College by Society   76
Presidential Stature   79

CHAPTER V

Personal and Professional Qualifications   82

Requirements of the College   82
Analysis of Personal and Professional
    Qualifications   85
Requirements and Previous Background   86
Personal Qualities   88
Need for Personal Recreation and Study   90
Analysis of Qualities Suggested by Those Who
    Are Holding or Who Have Held the Office   90

CHAPTER VI

The Vista   95

Bibliography   109

Index   113

The College President

CHAPTER I

Introduction

The impact of broadening spheres of knowledge has brought American colleges and universities into the daily lives of people to an extent inconceivable only a generation ago. Out of college laboratories are coming facts about human behavior, diet, sources of energy, and communication that are changing habits, enriching pleasures, and lengthening lives. Teams of researchers, in consultation with governmental and business officials, are exploring the resources of the oceans, extending the known boundaries of space, probing into the recesses of the mind.

An ever increasing percentage of college age youth is attending institutions of higher education. Campuses are increasingly the centers of community intellectual forums and cultural affairs. Colleges are accepting responsibilities of directional influence on national and international affairs. So important have institutions of higher education become that they well may be determining factors in the destiny of the world.

The dynamic role of colleges is such that people are becoming more attentive to and mindful of those who serve as their presidents. More should be known about the leaders of these most significant institutions. The tasks the presidents undertake, the responsibilities they bear, the nature of their jobs, and the kind of men they are— these questions demand attention as at no time in the past.

Historical Background

The American college presidency began with the election of Mr. Henry Dunster as chief officer of Harvard College in 1640. He received the title *president* which has continued at Harvard and has become the usual title for the chief executive of American institutions of higher education. But, as if to forewarn that there would be no consistency, at the beginning of the seventeenth century Harvard's head, Increase Mather, for a short time was called *rector*.

1

The roots of the early colleges, including Harvard, go back directly to British universities, in most cases the English ones. From there, the lineage of American higher educational organizations shares the common past which reaches back to the universities of the Middle Ages. It is notable, however, that the office of president today differs greatly from that of the contemporary chief executives of English colleges and universities. American colleges do not derive solely from English roots; the Scottish universities also furnished a number of ideas.

The transplanted seeds which were to sprout higher education on American soil carried characteristics peculiar to the period in which they were brought to the New World. After the Reformation, English colleges became more independent and grew in power at the expense of the central administration of the universities of which they were components. The prestige, size, and tradition of the universities allowed personnel to speak their minds with a freedom the Reformers sought to curb in the name of the new orthodoxy. The colleges were weaker and could more easily be controlled and so, paradoxically, a growth of their powers at the expense of the university was encouraged. The consequence was that the heads of the colleges also received increased authority. "It was in this period, when the presidential office was in the ascendant, that the first American colleges were founded." [1]

The peculiarities of the New World environment were a powerful influence on the fledging institutions. The colleges found themselves without the restraint of membership in a university. It proved impractical to duplicate the British universities' structure, because the sparsity of population necessitated scattering higher educational institutions along the Atlantic seaboard rather than concentrating them in a university organization. When many of them grew into true universities two hundred years later, the organizational changes took place below the level of the presidency, leaving that office and its powers far different from its European counterparts—if such may even be said to exist. The Americans did not establish a European style university head. Even when a model of the German graduate school was adopted in the latter part of the nineteenth century

---

[1] George P. Schmidt, *The Old Time College President* (New York: Columbia University Press, 1930), p. 57.

and superimposed on the basically English undergraduate college, the authority of the president was undiminished by importation of the German tradition of a weak university head.[2]

Probably for this reason virtually no distinction is to be made between the college and the university presidency. Even today nearly all the principles which govern the one apply to the other. As President Harold Stoke wrote, "Swarthmore College is obviously not the University of California, yet the president of Swarthmore does for his institution exactly what the president of California does for his."[3] In the minds of many, *college presidency* is the term applying to both offices.

Another distinctive aspect of the American college presidency also can be explained by circumstances in Colonial times: the control of the colleges by a board of men chosen from outside the professorate. Americans may owe the idea of a lay control board in part to the Scots.[4] The lay board of control developed as a natural consequence of sponsorship by religious denominations instead of by the established church of the European countries.[5] Members took on the responsibility in addition to their own vocations, with the result that they were hardly ever more than absentee overseers. The board necessarily relied on the president to assume executive responsibilities, because he was resident at the college and personally in touch with the day-to-day problems. The board's authority naturally came to be effectively centered in his office.

The presidents of higher institutions in the United States had and still have much greater influence and power than college heads in Europe. In extremely few instances has the president been the crea-

---

[2] For a treatment of the powers of administrators of universities in Imperial Germany before World War I, see Friedrich Paulsen, *The German Universities and University Study,* authorized translation by Frank Thilly and William W. Elwang (London: Longmans, Green, and Co., 1906).

[3] Harold W. Stoke, *The American College President* (New York: Harper & Brothers, 1959), p. 11.

[4] There is still debate on the extent to which William and Mary College may have borrowed the idea of control by a lay board rather than by the professorate. In this connection see John S. Brubacher and Willis Rudy, *Higher Education in Transition, An American History: 1936–1956* (New York: Harper & Brothers, 1958), pp. 4-5, and Richard Hofstadter and Walter P. Metzger, *The Development of Academic Freedom in the United States* (New York: Columbia University Press, 1955), p. 131, n. 30.

[5] The term *lay control* means the board members were not primarily educators; it is not used in the sense as *nonclerical.* In the early days especially, many board members were ordained ministers.

ture of the faculty. The board's delegation of authority to him in great part explains this.

Another peculiarity of Colonial America which contributed to the presidency's growth was the fact that teaching staff members seldom were permanent and had little professional cohesiveness. Many college instructors were young tutors who themselves had recently graduated and who had taken up teaching merely as temporary employment while waiting for other positions—more often than not in the ministry. Because teaching was regarded as a less desirable alternative, the president often would be one of the very few permanent members of a college staff. "The only secure and sustained professional office in American collegiate education was that of the college president himself." [6] It is no wonder that he came to be a dominant figure.

As if to prove that the autonomy of European faculties could not be transplanted, the organs which should have carried a strong faculty voice were transformed for other uses. In the case of Harvard, the Corporation had a faculty majority and stood between the Overseers and the college, but gradually its membership was closed to the teaching staff. At William and Mary, after a long period of contention the influence of the Masters was curbed and the lay Visitors exercised authority through the executive head.[7]

The title *president* has remained the most popular one in American usage since Dunster first assumed his Harvard office, but by no means is it uniformly employed. In the United States there are rectors, chancellors, and provosts whose duties clearly classify them with the college presidents. Virtually all these titles are based on a venerable history.

The title *rector* was used at Yale in the early years of the institution, possibly through a desire to be less pretentious.[8] There is ample support for this in European practice. Exeter and Lincoln Colleges of Oxford, for example, have rectors as their functioning heads, while the Scottish universities reserve the title for the top ranking office, chiefly an honorary one. On the continent—in France, Germany, and, usually, the Netherlands—*rector* is the

---

[6] Hofstadter and Metzger, *op. cit.*, p. 124.

[7] *Ibid.*, pp. 126-35; Brubacher and Rudy, *op. cit.*, pp. 30-31.

[8] Charles Franklin Thwing, *The College President* (New York: The Macmillan Company, 1926), p. 2. Thwing presents a section on the background of these titles, which has been drawn on.

usual title for the university head. This usage also is found at Madrid, Barcelona, Athens, and several Russian universities as well as those in Switzerland.

Rector as a title was first applied to civil officers and guild functionaries following the tradition of Roman law. The University at Bologna adopted the term from the guild,[9] and with the spread of Bologna's influence, it came to be commonly employed on the continent.

Often the power of the rector could be quite autocratic, as in the case of the rector at the University of Paris. In Scotland, however, both the rector and the chancellor today hold largely honorary positions. In Germany the rector holds office for a short period and has few powers compared to those of the college president in the United States.

Strangely enough, in some instances where the term *rector* did take root in the United States, the functions of the office are quite different from those across the Atlantic. At William and Mary both a rector and a chancellor were provided for in the charter of 1729, but neither of these officers was the chief executive. The rector was the head of the Board of Visitors, serving for a period of one year, and the term is still used to designate this official.

Chancellor also has been a term of limited but highly respectable employment in the United States. It was early connected with university institutions in Europe. In Paris the chancellor was a representative of the bishop, responsible for overseeing episcopal responsibilities with respect to the university and other schools. In the early days he was not a member of the organization's administration.[10] It came to be, however, that this clerical title was connected with several universities. At both Oxford and Cambridge there is a chancellor, but today the office is honorary and is largely without any administrative power.

The functioning heads of several American universities and colleges are called chancellors but only the title distinguishes them from the presidents. New York University, Syracuse, Pittsburg, Buffalo, Kansas, and Stanford have used, or are now using, this title

---

[9] Hastings Rashdall, *The Universities of Europe in the Middle Ages,* new edition edited by F. M. Powicke and A. B. Emden (London: Oxford University Press, 1936), I, 162-63.

[10] *Ibid.,* I, 305.

for their chief executive officer. The University of California uses "chancellor" for the executive heads of its campuses throughout the state, reserving the title of *president* for the head of the university as a whole. The state colleges of California provide direct contrast in this regard; each member institution is headed by a president subordinate to a single chancellor.

Provost also is a term of church origin. The title was given to the chief officer in a cathedral church school, who ranked second to the abbot. In the United States the provost has usually been a secondary officer in colleges and universities, but at the University of Pennsylvania it is the title of the institution's head. The term has been used or is in use for various positions at California, Yale, Johns Hopkins, and Columbia. At Columbia, the provost from 1811 to 1816 was an office superior to the presidency.

Whatever the title of their executive officers, the American colleges before the Civil War were closely connected with the churches, among whose principal educational concerns was the producing of an educated clergy. Since the best educated men of the time were ministers of the gospel, it was to be expected that college presidents would be of this calling.

There were few exceptions to this rule. In his study of *The Old Time College President,* George Schmidt examined the background of a large number of the early incumbents and concluded that nine-tenths of the college heads who served before the Civil War were ordained ministers. The few who were not took office after 1779. There was not a single lay president in the entire Colonial period. The only apparent exception to this may have been President John Leverett, who headed Harvard from 1708 to 1724. He is sometimes considered a layman, but this would appear a mere technicality as he was trained for the ministry and had preached on several occasions before turning to a career in law.[11]

Even after laymen began entering the presidential field, the barriers to nonclerics did not fall rapidly. In many cases a lay president was succeeded by another preacher. In 1850 the ratio of laymen to ministers was about the same as it was in 1800, approximately one to ten.[12]

The president's responsibilities were generally the same in all

[11] Schmidt, *op. cit.,* pp. 184-85.
[12] *Ibid.,* p. 185.

the early colleges. Schmidt has provided a summary of these duties. As might be expected, the college head presided at commencements and other ceremonies. He arranged morning and evening prayers as well as Sunday worship, and very likely led the service himself. In some cases he was required to conduct the faculty meetings. He was also expected to lecture on the "evidences of Christianity," and he might teach any other subject which he chose. He was supposed to visit the classes of other instructors—a requirement which has practically disappeared. Finally, he was required "to attend to the general superintendence and to promote the interests and reputation of the college by every exertion in his power." [13]

Often the president would be famous among his constitutents for his preaching, a circumstance which is not surprising in view of the fact that the early colleges were looked upon as an arm of the church. Today's president must be able to acquit himself at the rostrum with at least a modest degree of success; no doubt ability to perform well as a public speaker was demanded to a greater degree in early days.

A great deal of the difference between the activities of today's president and earlier presidents is explained by the fact that the colleges in the seventeenth and early eighteenth centuries were comparatively smaller institutions. In the period from Harvard's founding in 1636 to the end of the century only 465 students graduated, and the total in attendance for that whole period did not exceed 600. In the late eighteenth century Yale reached an enrollment peak with 415.

In institutions of such size there was every reason to expect the president to participate directly in most phases of the college's life. His disappearance from the immediate scene of most modern college activities is a consequence of the great growth of enrollments and curricula. The major function of the college staff was to teach. Here the president was expected to be involved personally, and he might teach more than one of the subjects offered. Today it is often not lack of teaching competence which keeps him from the classroom; it is simply that his other duties are so great that he cannot take time to instruct classes.

The most common course taught by presidents was a senior class

---

[13] *Ibid.*, p. 52.

in something usually called mental and moral philosophy. This could be about anything philosophical, and it was used to impress the president's views on the senior class. An analysis of the subject matter that went into this course will clearly indicate the cultural influence of the college president. Some presidents went so far in their desire to put their imprint on the graduates that they taught virtually the entire senior curriculum. Other presidents confined themselves strictly to a limited specialty, which might be literature, mathematics, Latin, or even science.

The president's educational influence certainly was not limited to his own class work. The institution's standards were largely a reflection of his determination to uphold them. Here the president's duties must have been very similar to those of contemporary presidents. He had to work indirectly through other faculty members and to struggle with such problems as recruiting of good instructors on a limited budget, maintaining morale in the face of pressures from all sides, and attracting superior students.

Today the collegiate institution puts great store in its objective of adding to human knowledge. This research function generally is regarded as one of the colleges' most important goals. It is now asserted more frequently than ever before that effective teaching must be accompanied by research investigation, a function almost completely unknown in the early American colleges. Professors then thought of themselves as teachers of what was known and felt content with competence in the classroom. Thus the president of those days was practically unconcerned with an area which today is demanding major attention. The modern president is required to have a genuine appreciation of research and to be a good judge of the men engaged in it.

Historically, one of the goals of the college has been the development of the student's character. Prior to the twentieth century, the president was at least as fully involved in this major educational preoccupation as he was in any other of the institution's goals. There are several very sharp differences between modern colleges and those of a hundred or three hundred years ago, and these differences go far to explain the changes in methods used for character development and the president's role in them. In the first place, the age of the college student two centuries ago was virtually that of the present high school student; the president was dealing with

teenagers rather than with young adults. Even the curriculum of
the past bore certain resemblances to today's secondary school curriculum. College students were very young until after the mid-
1800's; many were as young as twelve or thirteen and the college-
leaving age for most was about seventeen or eighteen. It was quite
normal, then, that President Willard of Harvard ordinarily greeted
students who approached him with "Well child, what do you
want?" [14]

The program to develop character was influenced not only by
the fact that the students were so young, but also by an educational
philosophy distinctly different from today's. The student's character
was to be formed through discipline. The rules he was obliged to
follow were, to be sure, an embodiment of high moral conduct as
well as good manners. Nevertheless, the philosophy of discipline of
the bygone era was markedly distinct from that presently current.
Many colleges were residential, and the student's life was a highly
regulated affair, with the president himself as the final authority.

"The student's life was that of a soldier in a barracks. He had a
fixed time for rising and retiring, ate at stated hours, and was required to spend certain periods of the day in study." [15] The regimen
was formulated by the trustees, and the president and his faculty
enforced it. Attendance at early chapel was usually an established
feature of the discipline-for-character-development pattern. Meals
in common were also generally an aspect of college life. Indulgence
in alcoholic beverages was prohibited, with certain attenuations of
rigor. At the University of Mississippi in 1848, liquor was prohibited unless the president gave his personal authorization. And at
William and Mary the prohibition on student drinking was modified
to the extent that students could indulge if they did not go beyond
that "which becomes the prudent and industrious student." [16] Numerous reports of student drunkenness make clear, however, that
college boys were far from careful to observe the regulations and
the problems engendered may have driven more than one administrator himself to drink.

Courtesy and propriety were inculcated through college rules,
and the figure of the president naturally loomed large as an object

---

[14] *Ibid.*, p. 78.
[15] *Ibid.*, p. 79.
[16] *Ibid.*, p. 80.

of respect. In the period before the Revolution, Princeton's students were obliged to raise their hats to the president at a distance of ten rods, while tutors could not expect to have students' hats tipped at such great distance—it was not considered too familiar to approach within five rods before making this gesture.

As the head of such a system, the president was patriarch as well as chief administrator. Not only did he have the sanction of the community in this role but he was sustained by a society much more accustomed to parental despotism than today's student can even imagine. One of the unwritten qualifications for a college presidency was that the man be the embodiment of the *pater familias*. His bearing, manner, and self-conviction had to conform squarely with this tradition if he were effectively to deal with the strains of office.

And strains there were, aplenty. Memoirs and letters of students in the days both before and after the Revolution make clear that student riots were known on virtually every campus. At Harvard the Commons witnessed a crockery battle between freshmen and sophomores in 1817 which ended only when all available dishes had been smashed. At commencement time in 1847, a visitor at Yale found the graduating class splintering the windows of their rooms. There was constant devilment on a smaller scale: innumerable presidential horses were given a coat of paint, and any number of cows were tied in chapels. There is no way of estimating the abuse which luckless tutors had to endure as a consequence of their being part of the authority of the institution. Some breaches of discipline were quite extreme, resulting in physical injury and great loss of property; in one of the most serious instances, a drunken student became infuriated during a heated political debate and actually killed the president.[17]

The college head had responsibilities and liabilities beyond the patriarchal. He had to maintain good relations with the college's governing board and his relationship with that body was of key importance to a successful administration. In many cases the chief executive held board membership, but this was by no means a universal arrangement. Initially, Yale and the University of Pennsylvania denied their presidents a seat on the board, and this example

---

[17] *Ibid.*, p. 86, referring to W. B. Sprague, *Annals of the American Pulpit* (New York: R. Carter & Brothers, 1859), IV, 590.

was followed by several lesser known and newer institutions. Experience seems to have dictated a different pattern, however; in the mid-eighteenth century the president of Yale was given *ex officio* membership, and the University of Pennsylvania eventually saw the wisdom of this closer contact and provided a board position for its president in the late nineteenth century.

It goes without saying that the president held his job only at the pleasure of the board. Differences of opinion either had to be anticipated and avoided, or thrashed out, or perhaps solved in the board's favor by the president's resignation. An early example of a rift between board and president resulted in the resignation of Increase Mather as head of Harvard in 1701. Congregationalist orthodoxy was the principal issue. A change in the composition of the board, resulting from political shifts in Massachusetts' ruling circles, allowed a broadening of the religious policy of the college. The president was a purist; rather than compromise to keep his job, he withdrew, and the Mather family transferred its allegiance and aspirations to Yale.[18]

The president's relationships with his faculty were virtually those of employer and employee, with the qualification that he himself was not a free agent because of his dependence on the ultimate support of the board of control. Since academic tenure, review of grievances, and faculty organizations to protect collective and individual rights were unknown in early college circles, presidents could be arbitrary and despotic. The skill and the restraint with which they used their authority was reflected in the quality of the school and, at times, in real hardships for individual victims of presidential wrath.

In the Colonial period, with a frequently changing instructional staff made up largely of young tutors, the president could dominate the institution if he was of a mind to do so. But in the better colleges shortly after the beginning of the nineteenth century there were signs that presidents consulted their faculties with a certain regularity. This was notably the case at Yale under Jeremiah Day whose presidency dated from 1817 to 1846. The history of faculty participation has not yet been compiled but apparently regular consultation with teaching colleagues was first established with respect

---

[18] Samuel Eliot Morison, *Three Centuries of Harvard, 1636–1936* (Cambridge, Mass.: Harvard University Press, 1936), pp. 45–50.

to new appointments. In the better institutions the instructional staff passed judgment on additions to its membership. But in numerous institutions, perhaps in most, presidential discretion alone determined who would be appointed.[19]

The number of presidents expanded greatly in the period of the Revolution and in the early nineteenth century. In 1780 there were only nine institutions of higher education in the United States. Up to the year of the outbreak of the Civil War, the country had a total of 182 colleges—all of which were destined to survive. But this shows only a part of the picture: over 400 institutions opened and failed within this period.[20] Whatever the insecurity of the teaching staff, no one could complain that the presidents were not sharing the risks. With the failure of a college, it is safe to say, a president was out of a job, at least for the time being. The great increase in number of institutions was due in large part to the driving passion of religious denominations to have their own colleges, especially to train their own ministry; the high mortality rate can be assigned to an excess of zeal over practical considerations. The presidents themselves often were ministers and could turn—slightly chastened —to the pulpit.

Regardless of what objections there may be to the powers of the early college presidency, the office clearly was one of the main instruments for advancement of higher education in the United States. A few able and farsighted presidents were responsible for initiating important changes. It must be said, however, that such leaders were a small minority, and generally suffered sharp criticism from other college administrators who felt innovations were bad for higher education.

One of the most remarkable of these leaders was Eliphalet Nott, who was president of Union College from 1804 to 1866, an astonishing span of sixty-two years. Nott liberalized the severe code of student discipline on the then alarming theory that students would be more responsible for their own conduct if the maintenance of discipline were not made a contest between student and faculty.

---

[19] Hofstadter and Metzger, *op. cit.*, pp. 233-36.

[20] Donald E. Tewksbury, *The Founding of American Colleges and Universities Before the Civil War with Particular Reference to The Religious Influences Bearing upon the College Movement*, Teachers College, Columbia University Contribution to Education, No. 543 (New York: Bureau of Publications, Teachers College, Columbia University, 1932), pp. 16, 28.

Nott went so far as to abstain from a gentlemen's agreement among college presidents to refuse admission to students expelled from other institutions for disciplinary reasons. He was one of the pioneers in introducing practical science courses into the tradition-bound curriculum of the early nineteenth century; in 1845 his college initiated a civil engineering program. Nott, along with very few others of his time, succeeded in raising the recitation method to the level of an instructive Socratic dialogue, thus triumphing over the deadly standard method which put the instructor in the role of listening to students report on what they had memorized from a book.

Often cited as the paragon of instructors was another unusual president, the highly gifted Mark Hopkins, who headed Williams College from 1836 to 1872. Hopkins, like Nott, was a pioneer disciplinarian. He mitigated the system of disciplinary fines and the constant policing of student conduct imposed on the faculty.

Inspired by contact with men such as Nott and Hopkins, a generation of college presidents attempted substantial improvements in higher education. Francis Wayland was one of the most influential. He had been a student of Nott's. As head of Brown University from 1827 to 1855, he liberalized the disciplinary regimen and notably advanced teaching through his own example. Unfortunately some of the advocates were ahead of their times. Henry Philip Tappan, first president of the University of Michigan, graduated from Union College in 1825 and was experienced in the methods advocated by Nott. When called to the presidency of Michigan in 1852, he not only drew on Nott's ideas, but endeavored to apply to Michigan some of the principles of the German universities. He eventually ran into resistance from the board of regents and was summarily dismissed. He left behind an unfulfilled program which became, at least in part, a blueprint for numerous higher educational institutions in later years.

President Jeremiah Day was an outstanding figure who left a lasting impact on higher education. He established the exceptional practice of consulting the faculty in important issues. Under his administration all new appointments went to the faculty for approval.

The last half of the nineteenth century saw extraordinary changes in higher education, and one can point to a handful of distinguished figures who seized the helm of educational leadership and contributed fundamentally to this development. These men were responding to the technological, social, and political changes which swept the country. But they were not merely finding answers to pressing demands; true leaders, they anticipated the country's needs and developed their aims through intimate understanding of higher education and real insight into its problems.

This was the period of the founding of such institutions as Johns Hopkins University and the University of Chicago, and the time when the movement to establish state universities was being carried from the South to the rest of the country. Johns Hopkins had its Gilman while Chicago had its Harper, and it is safe to say that neither institution could have advanced so rapidly without the unusual vigor of these presidents. But the older institutions found men of comparable stature such as Harvard's Eliot, who kept his institution at least abreast and often ahead of others.

Though the president historically has been regarded as a public figure, it is important to observe the limitations on his activities off the campus. Some presidents have been public figures of importance quite aside from their college positions, but presidential duties have not been combined with political or controversial activities. Few if any presidents have combined collegiate functions with significant political activity, and they are generally not expected to become seriously involved in politics. When a president engaged in really significant political activity, he eventually had to choose between his college post and his partisan leanings. President Low of Columbia, for example, resigned because of the trustees' disapproval of his desire to mix mayoralty campaigning with his university duties.

The more recent incumbencies of persons such as Harold Stassen do not mark a break in the nonpolitical tradition. They really signal the withdrawal of the politician from his former haunts, and attest to the dignity of the office by the fact that it is a very graceful exit from the public stage. Eisenhower's incumbency as university president did not serve quite the same function in his career as Stassen's had. Columbia was perhaps a suitable place to go after so many military honors, but his brief tenure also may have been very helpful in getting the public to think of him as someone other than a general. Several college and university presidents have gone on to try even greater responsibilities. One of the most notable of these was Woodrow Wilson. President Garfield, before his career as a general and President of the United States, served as principal of Western Reserve Eclectic Institute (later Hiram College).

The choice of a college president to perform duties unconnected with his institution has often been made primarily in order to obtain someone of unquestioned neutrality and impartiality. An example of this was the appointment of President Lowell of Harvard to a board to investigate grounds for pardoning Sacco and Vanzetti. Similarly, Van Hise of Wisconsin joined arbitration proceedings between railroadmen and their employees. The selection of a president for such tasks is one of the clearest indications of the prestige of the office.

Presidents have indeed played important leadership roles outside their own colleges, but these activities have been largely confined to the field of education. Charles W. Eliot and a handful of other distinguished presidents of the last half of the nineteenth century participated in numerous movements to improve American education. Certainly not all the presidents who sought to exert educational leadership were successful, because they occasionally desired opposed ends. Harper of Chicago fought for a reorganization of education so as to divide the college into junior and senior sections, but he succeeded only in part. The famous Committee of Ten, sponsored by the National Education Association, was composed largely of college presidents. The committee issued a report in 1893 dealing with the growing problems of articulation between the dual-purpose high school and the college. Though the report was criticized as being oriented in favor of the college preparatory course, it was an important document and is evidence of significant participation of college presidents in formulating overall education policy. Today it is standard for college presidents to be leading members of educational study commissions. Another example of presidential leadership is the service role of higher educational institutions, which was developed and propounded by Van Hise, president of the University of Wisconsin from 1903 to 1918.

The professions from which college presidents have been recruited became more and more numerous after the Civil War. The trend away from clerical presidents, which began in the period after the Revolution, accelerated rapidly after the Civil War. A large number of the later presidents came from various fields of scholarship. Eliot, inaugurated in 1869, was a professor and a scientist, though he succeeded to the presidential chair at so young an age that he never really distinguished himself for scientific contribution. Harper of Chicago was a noted scholar of Hebrew. G. Stanley Hall, president of Clark University in 1889, was outstanding in philosophy and psychology. David Starr Jordan, inaugurated as first president of Stanford in 1891, was a great naturalist. Princeton's first lay president, Woodrow Wilson, was a political scientist of some reputation. Michigan's James Burrill Angell, who took office in 1871, was a scholar in languages.

Today much is made over the fact that nonscholars may occupy the office of president. Some maintain that only a scholar will do for this post and that the holder of a medical degree or even a professional educational administrator should not be chosen. According to this notion, a military man or a businessman is *ipso facto* disqualified. Exceptions to this view are numerous and many have been successfully maintained. Washington and Lee University probably could not have been better served than it was by Robert E. Lee. It must be granted that Lotus Coffman, former superintendent of schools, served the University of Minnesota with great credit. In any event, the number of nonscholars has probably been exaggerated. At least one observer felt this when he stated:

> Practically all college administrators today have followed the traditional route from classrooms to deanships to presidencies. The number of businessmen, generals, or politicians in academic administration is negligible, if well dramatized.[21]

The question has been raised from time to time whether the college presidency is necessary at all. Certainly many presidents have been despotic enough and/or ineffective enough to encourage ideas of this kind. The fact that many European institutions have no office with comparable powers has always been an encouragement to those in this country who would experiment along similar lines. But even without overbearing presidents and the temptation of foreign examples, there is often a strong appeal to the academician in the idea that a community of intellectually sophisticated scholars can

---

[21] Robert J. Wert, "What Are the New Developments in the Preparation of College Administrators?" *Current Issues in Higher Education, 1959,* edited by G. Kerry Smith (Washington, D.C.: Association for Higher Education, 1959), p. 223.

handle their own problems efficiently through sheer force of logic. It was just such a conception of freedom that was behind the early organization of the University of Virginia, undertaken largely through Jefferson's inspiration. This movement was never successful; perhaps the president is not dispensable.

The Literature

When one considers how influential the collective corps of college presidents is for the United States, it is surprising that the literature on the office is so limited. It is true that the number of presidents at any one time is not large (there are slightly under 2,000), but the collective potential of these men and women to shape, or mis-shape, the future of the nation is tremendous. The main sources of information on this vital office are the writings of the presidents themselves. The publications which the busy leaders have had time for usually are memoirs and reflections written after the years of active service. In many ways, of course, it would be hard to find a better source of information, but these writings are necessarily limited by the fact that they represent the point of view of individuals whose personal experiences have been confined to small fractions of higher education. Nevertheless one must turn first to the practitioners themselves for the profession of the college president has not yet been the object of formal analysis.

One of the earliest books on the administration of higher education, *College Administration,* by Charles F. Thwing, appeared in 1900.[22] Thwing followed this study a quarter-century later with an admirable volume titled *The College President.* This has been succeeded by the writings of a few others. Harold Stoke, Henry Wriston, Herman Donovan, Frank McVey, and Raymond Hughes have made the most informative attempts at a full treatment of the subject, although they do not really claim so much to have written about the presidency as about their own experiences in office. Several very valuable collections of presidential speeches have shed a great deal of light on the speaker's office. An early one is *University Administration,* by Eliot, who lectured specifically on administration. Many published presidential speeches concerning the office

---

[22] The publications referred to in this section are cited in the Bibliography on p. 109.

of the presidency are designed to acquaint the public with particular institutions, thus making for a less objective approach. Among the most interesting of the recent publications is *Ongoing State University,* by Morrill of Minnesota, which tells a great deal about the state university but offers information on the presidency itself only indirectly. Chancellor Samuel Capen of the University of Buffalo has thrown some light on the problems with which the head of an urban institution of higher education must grapple. *The Management of Universities,* a collection of his speeches, is of special interest in the areas of higher education outside the liberal arts field. Another excellent compilation, by D. A. Weaver, contains inaugural addresses by presidents who served over twenty years.

A frank treatment of *The President of the Small College* is presented by Peter Sammartino of Fairleigh Dickinson University, who includes a number of valuable pointers on administrative techniques for such an institution. The most recent extensive study of the presidency is *The Academic President—Educator or Caretaker?* written by Princeton's president emeritus, Harold Dodds with the aid of a substantial grant from the Carnegie Corporation. This laudable undertaking offers some very interesting suggestions for improving the presidency which will be studied carefully in academic circles.

More numerous than presidential essays and speeches are the biographies of presidents. They offer much information, but they do not pretend to cover the subject of the American college presidency as such. Many of these biographies are undertaken as much in the interest of the former presidents' institutions as they are for the purpose of documenting the struggles of the men themselves. Consequently, here, too, a lack of candor on administrative problems is apparent. Nevertheless these biographies contain much that is useful to the study of the college presidency and, along with the autobiographical writings, are probably the most readable materials on the subject. Some of the best deal with the careers of Daniel Coit Gilman, William Rainey Harper, David Starr Jordan, Charles A. Eliot, and A. Lawrence Lowell.

Administrators who have not been presidents have written significant observations on higher education. At least they present valuable insights into the presidential role, even if they do not cover the subject systematically. Jacques Barzun, Provost of Columbia University, has very effectively presented his views on the state of higher education. The volume by Monroe Deutsch ably expresses the view of a man with a fine appreciation of the virtues of scholarship and the need for academic freedom. His observation that the first duty of a president is educational leadership is especially persuasive. In a book titled *Principles of College and University Administration,* Dean Lloyd Woodburne has undertaken one of the very few administrative studies of higher institutions.

The wider aspects of administrative leadership are presented in a number of works not concerned specifically with the college presidency. Some of the most stimulating are by Marshall E. Dimock, Ordway Tead, and Philip Selznick. The stimulating writings of educator-philosopher Frederick Mayer, especially his *Creative Universities,* draw attention to the educational administrator's responsibilities. Thomas Blackwell has presented a very useful summary of college law, well documented and replete with succinct summaries of significant cases. The college president inevitably will find this work useful in understanding the institution and tradition entrusted to him.

The lack of an integrated analysis of the office of the president has its counterpart in the lack of specific preparation of the presidents themselves. Up to the present there have been only limited efforts to provide formal training for the man who has assumed or is about to assume this leadership role. An approach to such a program is currently being provided under the directorship of Professor Robert Merry at Harvard, where a summer institute is held for newly appointed presidents.[23] Until such time as formal training is regularly provided for men with presidential ambitions and potential, colleges and universities must continue to provide their leaders with on-the-job training in their duties and responsibilities.

---

[23] For a brief discussion of this organization see p. 104.

CHAPTER II

Nature of the Office

Traditions of the Office

The college presidency has an individuality which the person who holds the office must accept and foster if he hopes to meet its responsibilities successfully. Certainly the demands are great. As Henry Wriston commented on his presidential career, "Into every life some rain must fall, and there were times when I thought I would drown." [1]

After accepting the challenge of the office, the incumbent encounters strange paradoxes. He receives recommendations for action from many sources: his administrative associates, the teaching faculty, the students, the alumni, the patrons of the college. If he takes action in contradiction to a recommendation, he is guilty of a liberty which legally is his but morally may not be.

Does the college president have the moral right to deny the recommendation of a committee on a subject of an academic nature? Representatives of the teaching faculty, for example, may insist, "The faculty should have major responsibility for the educational and research policy of the institution." [2] Is the office of president one of passive or dynamic leadership? If the leadership is dynamic, is it in keeping with the academic tradition to veto actions which may have the support of a majority of the students or the faculty? How is the office of president viewed by students, faculty, and alumni? If on the one hand the presidency is to be like the office of rector of the German university, then the president is more passive than dynamic. He is expected to shoot straws into the wind, as it were. If the current of feeling on the campus approaches unanimity and it is evident that academe is vitally interested in an issue, then

---

[1] Henry M. Wriston, *Academic Procession, Reflections of a College President* (New York: Columbia University Press, 1959), p. 116.

[2] The Association's tentative statement of principles is published under the title "Faculty Participation in College and University Government," *AAUP Bulletin*, XLVI, No. 2 (June, 1960), p. 204.

the president follows the judgment of the majority and the authority of his office is used simply to implement the action.

On the other hand, if the American college presidency has a distinct character of its own and is truly reflected in the activities of Eliot of Harvard, Harper of Chicago, Cotton Mather of Yale, Angell of Michigan, Wayland of Brown, and Hall of Clark, then the college president should play a more vigorous role, and his decisions will reflect his own strong moral convictions.

However the president's office is viewed, there are noteworthy examples of the distinction which the position has come to hold. *Who's Who in America* includes the names of college presidents by virtue of the office they hold, an honor given to only a few other persons.[3] A status classification by Mid-Western college and high school students shows clearly that the college presidency ranks very high as compared with other positions. Only five other occupations were ranked higher: Supreme Court Justice, U.S. Ambassador, Cabinet Secretary, U.S. Senator, and state governor. Big city bankers, mayors, and medical doctors all ceded place to the college president.[4]

The college presidency has attracted noted men from many fields. It has held out the hope that in this position a goal may be reached, a cause may be nurtured, the truth may finally be brought to light. To Horace Mann the presidency of Antioch College seemed a means of climaxing his dream to do for higher education what he had so successfully done for the lower schools during his distinguished career in many responsible positions in Massachusetts.[5] To William Rainey Harper the presidency of the University of Chicago provided an opportunity to apply unique theories about organizing the college experience for the learner. It is suggested that one of his experiments

---

[3] In addition to persons listed because of authorship, the following are other categories of positions deemed prestigious enough so that their incumbents are automatically listed in *Who's Who:* members of Congress; Cabinet members; Federal judges; Governors of states, territories, and island possessions; judges of state and territorial courts of highest appellate jurisdiction; Ambassadors and Ministers of the United States and those accredited to the United States; members of certain national academies (science, design, and arts and letters); and members of the National Institute of Arts and Letters.

[4] Mapheus Smith, "An Empirical Scale of Prestige Status of Occupations," *American Sociological Review,* VIII, No. 2 (April, 1943), pp. 185-92.

[5] Joy Elmer Morgan, *Horace Mann at Antioch* (Washington, D.C.: National Education Association, 1938), p. 60.

was a major force in the development of the junior college.[6] Increase Mather became president of Harvard because the position promised to give greater influence to his preaching.[7] To Robert A. Milliken, the chairmanship of the executive council of California Institute of Technology presented an opportunity to realize a goal for preparing outstanding leadership for the fields of science and engineering.[8]

General Robert E. Lee, after the Civil War, accepted the presidency of the institution now known as Washington and Lee University so that he might help direct the education of leaders who would assume the task of reuniting the North and the South.[9] Charles W. Eliot declared at his inauguration as president of Harvard that he was committed to the elective system.[10] Henry Philip Tappan was so certain that the vertical expansion of the curriculum held the future promise for American universities that he tenaciously battled for his beliefs during his twelve years' incumbency at the University of Michigan.

It is debatable to what extent the special ambitions of deeply committed men have been realized in the time they have been college presidents, but most of those who have accepted the challenge have found it demanding, even exhausting. Harold Stoke wrote that it is probably such characteristics as these which have made the college presidency attractive to those who are eager to try it. He points to further paradoxes of the office:

> . . . those who enjoy it are not very successful, and those who are successful are not very happy. The explanation is hidden somewhere in the philosophy of power. Those who enjoy exercising power shouldn't have it, and those who should exercise it are not likely to enjoy it. One thing is clear: colleges must have presidents and it makes a great difference who they are! [11]

There is no doubt that many distinguished college presidents have left their marks on the office, but there is equal evidence that the

---

[6] Frederick Eby, *The Development of Modern Education, in Theory, Organization, and Practice,* 2d ed. (Englewood Cliffs, N. J.: Prentice-Hall, Inc., 1952), p. 594.

[7] "Increase Mather," *Dictionary of American Biography* (1935), XII, 390-94.

[8] "Robert A. Milliken," *Encyclopaedia Britannica* (1956), XV, 500.

[9] "Robert E. Lee," *Encyclopedia Americana* (1956), XVII, 185-88.

[10] Charles William Eliot, "Educational Reform," inaugural address at Harvard, *Builders of American Universities,* edited by David Andrew Weaver (Alton, Ill.: Shurtleff College Press, 1950), I, 24.

[11] Stoke, *op. cit.,* p. 20.

office has made even the strongest-willed among its occupants bend to the traditions which have grown up around it. The president's own individuality is caught up in the presidential role and to a degree is assimilated in the image of that office held by the public. He speaks for the campus. He represents authority in the minds of the faculty. He is the giver and taker away in the minds of the students. His behavior and his thoughts, as indicated in his public or private statements, are seized upon as the viewpoint of the institution. He is saint, satan, and somnambulist, depending on the favor he grants or denies.

The College President as Others See Him

To most students, after he delivers his welcoming speech, the president is a dim figure. Except for the fact that the modern president is probably clean shaven, they will recall him as Wriston did when he looked back on his own undergraduate years: "Bearded, dignified, remote, absent from the campus most of the time, he moved in an orbit far removed from mine." [12]

During the student's undergraduate years the president may be the cause of several frustrations in thwarting the more exuberant projects of young collegians. Yet, occasionally he may be the giver of cherished privileges, such as an unexpected holiday—celebration of a conference title or extension of a spring festival.

A few students, those who hold campus offices and have leadership positions in college affairs, may come to know the president personally. To such students the president is no longer a remote figure or a symbol of authority, and their impressions of his personality are conveyed to students with whom they associate.

When a student is ready to graduate, he once again sees the president in sharp focus and centers upon him a sentimental attachment for alma mater. When the president declares the traditional formula "By virtue of the authority vested in me I confer upon you the degree . . .", as Harold Stoke rightly observes, "He speaks for all higher education, for the faculty who certify the competence of the students, for the trustees who have vested their authority in him, and for the society whose support, public or private, maintains the institution." [13] Surely even though their personal contacts with the

---

[12] Wriston, *op. cit.*, p. 4.
[13] Stoke, *op. cit.*, pp. 1-2.

president have been rather limited, the graduating seniors include the presidential person as one of the memorable figures in their college experience.

In most church-related colleges the president is expected to conform to the tenets of the devout churchgoer. If the college is a technical institution, the president is expected to be conversant with the great skills which are incorporated in the major curricula. If the college is a liberal arts institution, the president is expected to have a broad educational preparation and erudite views on many subjects. In short, the president is expected either to exemplify the ideals of the institution or to be the spokesman for its point of view. This is the role he plays in the minds and eyes of the students.

After the student becomes an alumnus, he views the president differently. The president is no longer a symbol of the college. He may no longer seem so erudite, nor so aloof, nor, in some respects, such a mythical person. He is far more real a person than had been supposed, one with many of the common misgivings and some of the doubts of others. In short, he is human!

Alumni come to regard the president of the college as a resource person. He is the liaison between the alumni association and the college. He is the key figure in alumni development. He is the best drawing card at alumni meetings, for he is the one who speaks with the most commanding voice of the past glories and future ambitions of the college. He is the maker of plans. He is the giver of favors. He is the one who always duns alumni for money. To alumni in the legislature, he is the one who is continuously in need of "your help" in order that alma mater may have her budget favorably considered. The president is also the one who asks the alumni to recruit in their community the finest young people for the college.

Some of the alumni become reasonably well acquainted with the college president when he attends alumni institutes and workshops or performs as the ringmaster on extensive alumni tours. On these occasions the president has a key role in bringing the college to the alumni. Often such tours will take several weeks and may reach a number of important metropolitan areas in the state, if the institution is a state supported college, or may visit the cities of a whole region, if it is a private institution. The theme of such alumni conclaves is generally the same: what is alma mater now doing, what are her needs, and what are the great plans for her future? Many alumni attend these affairs hoping to recapture some of the excitement and thrills they had as students, and some may come to offer service or give advice on the management of the college.

To the faculty the president is the symbol of authority. He *is* the administration. He is the enforcer of the rules, and some say he has the image of management. Generally, the faculty is sensitive to his presence. Restraint normally prevails when the president converses with the faculty. He imposes a certain air of formality and, depending somewhat on his personality, also a feeling of reserve, or on some occasions even arouses a kind of wholesome respect. His approval is most welcome if it comes in response to something that the faculty member regards important. If the affairs of the institution are not going well, the president inevitably is viewed with some irritation. He can console himself that he is usually not the sole source of irritation to the faculty, even though he may be held responsible by the community for everything that takes place on the campus. Too frequently, however, the faculty does credit the president with the authority to correct anything or anyone "if he wants to."

All that has been said about the college president is modified appreciably by the personality of the person in the office. Generally, in the eyes of the students, the alumni, and the faculty, the man and his office are one. If the president is a reserved person, then the reaction to his office is quite different from what it would be were he an affable fellow. Unavoidably, however, similar pressures produce similar reactions. College presidents tend to act somewhat alike by virtue of the similarity of the problems which confront them from day to day, and these special kinds of problems make the college presidency unlike other leadership posts in American life.

Perhaps it is for these reasons that he especially enjoys the company of his fellow college presidents. The restrictions, the disposition to be on guard, and the shackles of authority fall away. Here a spirit of camaraderie prevails, and the president becomes a very different person in this company from the one he is on campus.

Nevertheless, it is to be expected that among the presidents, as among the colleges and universities themselves, there is a competition of the fiercest kind. Among presidents of public colleges there is rivalry for legislative appropriations, and it is not uncommon for some to unite against others of their company to get more of the state's resources. Private college presidents vie for favors and funds from benefactors. Competition for noted scholars as faculty members and for honor graduates as students also spark presidential combats. Out of this rivalry, which is usually turbulent but fair, frequently has come a better college and a better president. Harvard's reputation was enhanced during the presidency of Eliot. It cannot be doubted that the institution gained greatly by its competition with Columbia, Pennsylvania, and Yale for educational leadership. Johns Hopkins, under the presidency of Gilman, threatened Harvard's preëminence. About the same time Michigan became a great state university under Angell, while California and Minnesota under Wheeler and Coffman challenged Michigan.

> Meanwhile the University of Chicago staggered the academic world with the masterful plans of the dynamic William Rainey Harper who knew exactly where he wanted to go and had the ability to pyramid John D. Rockefeller's original benefaction of $600,000 to a score of a million before he died at the youthful age of forty-nine.[14]

Small colleges too have been blessed with highly competitive and successful presidents, among them Arthur E. Morgan at Antioch, William DeWitt Hyde at Bowdoin, William T. Foster at Reed, and Frank Aydelotte at Swarthmore.

Some may compare the college president to a chameleon who changes color to fit a part he plays, but such exaggeration presents a distorted picture. A vignette points up some special characteristics of the office. The college president on one campus of considerable reputation is regarded as a very authoritarian-centered administrator. He alone makes all the decisions, or at least he is credited with doing so. He does not seek advice or counsel; he only receives it when it is offered. He accepts what he chooses and rejects without ceremony that which does not appeal to him. He skillfully uses all political avenues available to him and his institution. His term of office has been so long that his personality is inseparable from the historical growth of his institution; he is indeed the one person in his college who stands between the source of light and the shadows. Fortunately, his ideas have been very good, and his prestige is now unquestioned. Among his fellow presidents he is affable, friendly,

---

14 W. H. Cowley, "What Does a College President Do?", an address presented at the inauguration of Roy E. Lieuallen as President of Oregon College of Education, Feb. 5, 1956 (n.p., 1956?), pp. 18-21.

considerate, and gracious. He has an endless supply of anecdotes and a warm and inspiring personality. There is no indication that he could be a despot, however benevolent. It is quite probable that some college presidents have indeed played a part in the drama of their colleges similar to that of Augustus Caesar, and that their institutions have benefited from this outright *imperium*. Even though they are anomalies in a democratic society, they may well ask, like Augustus at the end of his reign: "Have I not played my part well?"

The President as Interpreter and Defender of Aims

No person on the college campus is more nearly the interpreter of the philosophy of the campus than is the president. Hutchins declared that the highest function of the administrator is to clarify or to discover the mission of his college.[15]

The president speaks of the mission of his college—yes, even the philosophy of his campus—often with only the partial concurrence of many of the faculty or perhaps even of segments of the Board of Control. There can never really be an end to the debate about the mission of the college because a college never reaches an end point. It is a living institution and its goals and philosophy must constantly be in a state of evolution and growth. This evolution prevents unanimity because not every member of a faculty will have the same appreciation of the development of subject areas and society. This is all the more reason why the president must keep laboring away in his function of defining the mission of his college.

In communicating this mission and carrying it out, the college president works almost exclusively with professional people. The goal of the institution is carried out directly by the faculty. Harold Stoke observed that there is great truth in the cliché: "No college or university is better than its faculty." [16] In recruiting new members, the president must be especially attentive to the fact that the institution's aims will be expressed through them. He should not completely delegate the recruitment responsibility if he can possibly avoid doing so, because of its intimate relationship to the responsibility for setting the mission of the whole institution. The moment

---

[15] Robert Maynard Hutchins, "The Administrator: Leader or Office Holder," *Journal of Higher Education,* XVI, No. 8 (Nov., 1946), pp. 395-96.

[16] Stoke, *op. cit.,* p. 106.

of decision in appointing a faculty member is always an important stroke in shaping the college to its mission. One measure of a president's success in appointing new faculty is the perspective which time gives—has the stroke miscarried, has it generally contributed to the form, or has it hewn deeply and truly to the mark? Does the new faculty member enthusiastically associate himself with the goals and philosophy of the college? The truly rewarding achievement in the recruitment efforts of the president is a new faculty member who gives fresh inspiration in developing and disseminating the vision of the mission of the institution.

The faculty, conscientiously busy at the work of the college, is too frequently the target of destructive criticism. When the college is attacked unfairly, it is the president's obligation to speak out militantly in its defense. He must be in the forefront of the fight for freedom—freedom with responsibility. The college campus is and should be the place where ideas are welcome, be they comforting or provocative. It is the place for the innovator. It is a place where the search for truth must be unchallenged, but the concept of responsibility poses a fine line of adjustment between freedom and license.

The president himself must encourage the unbiased reflections of the competent scholars on his campus with respect to the issues of the day, and off-campus he must speak out for unshackled freedom in the pursuit of truth. He may not agree with the point of view but, with Voltaire, he must adamantly insist that there be no coercion toward conformity or suppression of ideas. Foremost among the institutions of democracy are the schools and colleges, and the enemies of the democratic process would undermine it most effectively by discrediting its basic institutions. In order that this freedom to judge and foster the truth be preserved in the colleges and universities, it is often necessary for the president to defend the minority. He should carry the conviction that if a man—a thoughtful man —has something to say, he should be heard. His thinking may be contrary to the popular view, even in conflict with the most influential forces of the society. But who knows? The innovator, the challenger, the doubter, may be right. New ideas, especially radically new ideas, may be abrasive or irritating and may arouse an almost irrational reaction, but given time and an opportunity for defense, the new idea may be the solution to a serious situation. This is the concept that directs the efforts of the college. This is the freedom for which the president must always be prepared to do battle.

In communications a dictum that merits frequent repetition is, "If it is possible to be misunderstood, you will be misunderstood." The president is frequently in the position of the swimmer who is required to tread water: his most vigorous efforts may only keep him afloat. His position on the campus and off is an unwavering insistence on fair play. The way in which he expresses his thoughts has an important bearing on the manner in which they will be received. The president is not free to speak his mind on the topics of the day. He is not free to indulge in rumor or sarcasm. He is taken literally. He is the guardian of the traditional role of the college in its search for truth. He is a spokesman for the ideals of higher education.

The President and the Board of Control

The college president has a major responsibility for establishing proper rapport with the board of control. Whether the board is appointed by the state governor or elected by the people, the college president usually serves as its executive officer.

Private colleges often have self-perpetuating boards and some private and a few publicly supported colleges or universities have unusually long staggered terms for board members. In such institutions the relationship between the president and the board is somewhat different from that in a college governed by trustees who have short terms and probably are not reappointed. The president may be the executive officer of the board, or even a member of it, but a majority of the board members have years of experience in their roles and his influence may be more subtle, less evident and direct.

Whether the composition of the board is subject to frequent change or not, the president's duties are essentially the same. He is the primary source of information from the campus communities; he interprets the needs, documents the requests, and presents the problems, achievements, and shortcomings of the college in an honest and factual way. He conveys the directions and decisions of the board to the campus. He is the liaison officer between the board and the college, and he facilitates the functioning of the board. He must recognize that the board is the source of authority and has the final responsibility in policy matters and decision-making.

The board should meet often enough to fulfill its responsibility properly. It should limit its activity to formulating policy and evaluating the success of the college. The board must hold the president accountable for proper administration, and it should require the submission of reports and documents which will help it in its work. Representative committees of faculty and students may meet with the board periodically because, as interpreter of the college to lay groups, the board should have firsthand experience with the teaching faculty and student associations.

It is the prerogative of the board to formulate the extent and limit of the president's authority. It may decide to take an active part in the management of the college and delegate limited authority to the president, or it may choose to delegate its authority generously. In any case, it is the president who is held responsible for the proper management of the campus, and one of his primary duties is determining the best means of working with the trustees. Usually the president's status and general duties are defined in the by-laws or regulations of the board.

Legal status of the office. If any conclusion may be drawn as to a definition of the legal status of the college president, it is that specificity may range from the merest reference to the president's office to a detailed exposition of his responsibilities in the regulations of governing boards.

In order to assess the situation, a questionnaire was addressed to the chief legal officer and the chief education officer of the fifty states in the Union. Their replies revealed that no clear indication as to the legal status of this office is to be found in constitutions, statutes, or administrative regulations. It may, however, be concluded that generally the state college or university president does not enjoy tenure status. In the vast majority of states, he is the appointee of the governing board of the institution and serves at its pleasure, being reappointed year to year or on some other terminal contract basis.

Few states (Illinois, Kentucky, North Carolina, North Dakota, and Oregon) offer the security of tenure to presidents of their institutions of higher learning. At least two states (Iowa and Wisconsin) grant tenure as professor to those presidents who hold professorial rank. And two others (Kentucky and North Carolina) grant tenure to the president of the state university but provide fixed terms for the administrative head of teachers colleges or normal schools.

Nor do many states make explicit provision regarding qualification for the office of the presidency of collegiate institutions. Among those that do, one (Illinois) requires that the president of each university shall hold an earned doctorate.

Two states (Massachusetts and Nebraska) require their college presidents to furnish bond for faithful performance, with one of these (Nebraska) also requiring its presidents to have a degree from a college or university recognized as equal in rank to those having membership in the Association of American Universities.

The unusual provision that the "board shall take care that the president of the university shall not be an atheist or infidel" is found in another state (South Carolina).

Membership on the board of control of his institution is assured the presidents of certain of their colleges and universities by nine states (Colorado, Connecticut, Hawaii, Michigan, Nevada, North Carolina, Texas, Utah, and Wyoming) in a constitutional provision, statute, or administrative regulation.

Also by statute or board regulation, the president may be designated chairman of the faculty senate (Colorado), *ex officio* chairman of the faculty (Georgia), president of the faculty (Michigan), principal officer of the faculty (Minnesota), or executive head of the university and presiding officer of the faculty (Nevada).

By provision of the administrative code, the president of one state university (Oregon) is given the right to preside over the legislative body of his faculties and the right to veto their decisions (the veto is subject to review by the chancellor).

The veto of faculty actions by the state university president in another state (Idaho) is subject to review by the board of control upon a referendum of three-quarters of the faculty or academic council.

Whether by board regulation or statute, it is clear that generally the trustees of a college expect the president to preside at faculty meetings, take an active part in committee deliberations, and exercise such influence on academic affairs as will enable the college to fulfill its mission. Although it is sometimes contended that trustees are interested primarily in the managerial ability and the public relations success of the president, most boards of control want a president who is part of and understands *academe*.

Selection of a college president.   The selection of a president for an institution of higher education is one of the most, if not the most, important duties of a board of trustees.

The process by which the new president is chosen varies greatly. The manner in which the trustees carry out this responsibility depends on the college and on the experience and wisdom of the board. John J. Corson reports an analysis of the procedures by which three university boards (Princeton, Toledo, and Virginia) made presidential selections during 1959. He stated:

> 1. Each board formulated an explicit or implicit statement about the kind of individual they sought. In two institutions the lay board members clearly indicated that they sought a scholar (preferably from their own institution) and manifested little concern with prior administrative experience. In one institution, Toledo, the board squarely stated that it wanted an educational administrator, *i.e.,* an individual trained as a scholar who had had administrative experience as a departmental chairman, as a dean, as the president of another institution, or in a similar position. There they obtained a man with substantial administrative experience.
>
> 2. Each board followed a simple procedure in seeking nominees for the post. The alumni were politely invited to offer suggestions. The faculty's views were invited in two institutions. Foundation officers and executors of educational associations were visited and their suggestions solicited. Many other university presidents, *e.g.,* Henry M. Wriston and Harold W. Dodds, were canvassed by letter or telephone. Lay board members, lacking familiarity with personnel in other institutions, sought widely the advice of professionals in the field, on whom they relied for the evaluation of men whose skills in the educational field they were not adequately equipped to appraise.
>
> 3. The part the faculty was invited to play in two institutions— Princeton and Virginia—was a large one; in Toledo the faculty was accorded little or no part. In the former institutions committees of the faculty assisted the boards at the start in formulating criteria for the kind of men wanted. They recommended men for the boards' consideration, and reviewed and commented on other individuals whose names were brought to the boards' attention.[17]

---

[17] John J. Corson, *Governance of Colleges and Universities* (New York: McGraw-Hill Book Company, Inc., 1960), pp. 53-4.

One possible plan would have as its first step a careful analysis of the needs of the campus seeking a president. This should be a self-study by representatives of campus groups and by representatives of the board of control. The assistance of an outside consultant can be advantageous because it lessens the possibility of precipitous advancement of favorite candidates by on-campus contingents. This exploratory phase should consider the institution's strengths and shortcomings. If the situation is a contentious one, the study committee should be headed by an experienced outsider who under no circumstances would be a candidate himself.

After the analysis is made, the same committee or another one with representatives from the original committee would be appointed to receive, analyze, and screen the proposed candidates. This group should consist of probably not more than seven, and preferably five, members. It will be able to work with a greater freedom if the membership is unrevealed except to the board. Before the committee is designated, a public statement should make clear that it will contain representation of the faculty, the alumni, and the board of control; but until the task has been completed, the names should not be announced. All the papers concerning candidates should go to one office—probably the office of the chairman of the board—and forwarded from that office to the committee.

When the vacancy is announced, there should be a clear statement of the conditions of the contract, such as salary, length of term, areas of authority and responsibility, and selection of administrative subordinates. Serious contenders should be informed of the extent to which authority traditionally has been delegated by the board. To assure objectivity and a broad base for selection, it would be wise not to exclude candidacies from the campus nor to limit the search to those on the campus.

It is not likely that a new president in an established college will have an opportunity to choose many of his administrative colleagues. Deans generally will have tenure or other guarantees and, consequently, the president will not have a free hand with them. One of the new president's greatest problems may be that he is expected to implement new policies but is unable to because the other administrators are permanent fixtures. To prevent this impasse, deans and other members of the administrative faculty should have tenure in teaching. This would enable them to continue with the institution they have served and at the same time allow the new president to make changes necessary to carry out his responsibility.

When serious contenders for the presidential post are found, they should first be interviewed in noncompromising places. If they are engaged in college teaching or administration, the interview should be away from their own campus and certainly away from the campus seeking the new president. When the candidates have been reduced to a small number, probably three, an interview as searching as discretion will permit should take place with each candidate at his place of employment. The final candidates may then be invited to the campus seeking the new president. It would be wise in most cases to keep the identity of finalists confidential to protect the future status of those not selected.

When all this has been accomplished, the committee should present the entire board of control with a list of the candidates in order of preference. It is important that the entire board participate in the selection. The finalists should be candidly interviewed by the board members and an offer made as soon as possible.

This plan can have great advantage if the screening committees are constituted of persons who enjoy the confidence of the whole college community.

A board of trustees may expect to seek a new president every eight years or so. The years of service of college presidents range from 5.8 for Catholic institutions (where rotation in office is an accepted policy) to 9.7 years for teachers colleges, both public and private.[18] After completing the demanding task of selecting a president, the trustees will probably agree with the conclusion of a faculty committee serving the board of regents in one of the major universities: ". . . in order to have an administration with substantial achievement, particularly in view of the initial slowness in getting a grip on the job, a substantial length of tenure is desirable." Furthermore the longer contractual agreement may preclude the ". . . early necessity of finding a successor." [19]

---

[18] William K. Selden, "How Long is a College President?", *Liberal Education*, The Bulletin of the Association of American Colleges, XLVI, No. 1 (March, 1960), pp. 5-15.

[19] "Tentative Thoughts Concerning Desirable Qualifications for a University of California President," unpublished draft approved by the Academic Senate Advisory Committee on the Selection of a President, Berkeley, April 9, 1957.

The men chosen may be persons with great variety of experience and background. In point of fact, however, there are numerous similarities among newly appointed presidents. Richard W. Stephens has found enough of a pattern among newly elected presidents of large colleges and universities to draw up a composite picture. This imaginary person was born and reared in a small town and has a bachelor of arts degree from a small liberal arts college where he earned membership in Phi Beta Kappa. The chances are good that his academic major was in history, economics, or perhaps English and that he has one or more advanced degrees from Harvard, Chicago, or Yale. He is a Rotarian, or a Kiwanian, a Republican, a war veteran, a legionnaire, and a Mason. He is married, and his family includes two or three adolescent or grown children; he and they are Episcopalians, Methodists, or Unitarians. The new president likes fishing or golf and has been abroad one or more times. He has written for publication occasionally and is the author of one or more books.

Most university and college presidents have had previous administrative experience, probably as deans, but a few have come from public school administration and from business. "Contrary to popular belief, the proportion of presidents selected from occupations outside higher education does not seem to have increased materially since 1900." [20] Smaller universities and liberal arts colleges have a higher percentage of presidents with no administration experience. There has been a general tendency for both large and small institutions to draw presidents from the ranks, which has led some observers to discern the development of a career pattern.[21]

There has also been an increasing number of presidents with earned doctorates, but the figure is lower for the smaller institutions. Approximately 68 percent of university presidents have earned doctorates, whereas the average of Stephens' sample from collegiate institutions of all sizes was 61 percent.[22] Although the presidents of the larger institutions tend to have studied the social sciences, presi-

---

[20] Richard W. Stephens, "The Academic Administrator: The Role of the University President" (Ph.D. dissertation, University of North Carolina, Chapel Hill, N. C., 1956), p. 85.

[21] C. H. Page, "Bureaucracy in Higher Education," *Journal of Higher Education* II (Jan., 1951), p. 96.

[22] Stephens, *op. cit.*, p. 87.

dents of smaller colleges or universities are most likely to have studied education or theology.[23]

The multi-campus board of control. The administration of two or more colleges under a single board of control is a growing development in public higher education. The presidents of such colleges commonly are responsible to the board's executive officer, and, although administrative duties are not appreciably different from those of presidents directly responsible to lay boards, some special considerations are involved. Freed from direct involvement with the legislature at fund-raising time, benefiting from the greater economy possible in a larger unit of control, and profiting from the findings of a better staffed research center, the president of such an institution has more time and energy for on-campus affairs and has resources of information and consultation among his counterparts at member colleges. He is also challenged to meet the achievements and standards of the best college in the system.

Possible frustrations resulting from membership in a system can be lessened by regular and frequent meetings between the central administrator and the presidents of the colleges. Once administrative policy has been determined, a considerable degree of autonomy can be exercised.

Doubtlessly disadvantages may be present in these systems. The college president suffers a delimitation of his decision-making authority, and there is a psychological disadvantage in his not being the last link in the chain of command. Other campus officials may become impatient with procedural delays. To a limited degree, also, member institutions suffer some loss of individuality.

With rapidly expanding collegiate enrollments and increasing concern for greater economies, quite probably more states will devise larger administrative units in an effort to obtain greater efficiency. Whether their objectives will be realized remains to be seen. Present evidence is inconclusive. A college president who is fearful of the trend toward consolidation and coordination may find reassurance in the fact that many of his colleagues with experience in these systems have endorsed this trend. No matter how great the advantages may be, the initial adjustments are numerous

---

[23] The sample did not include teachers colleges. Stephens, *op. cit.*, Table 4, p. 90.

and the period of transition from independence to integration can be unsettling.

The Duties of the Office

Authorities and research workers who have written about the college presidency agree it is a most varied and demanding responsibility. W. H. Cowley believes the four major categories of presidential duties include superintending, facilitating, developing, and leading.[24] In each of these areas there is further diversity of responsibilities. A former college president wrote:

> To be effective, the faculty must look to the president to do three things: to state the ends which the college and hence the faculty are trying to serve, and to set the tone of the enterprise; to provide the means which will enable the faculty to do its work well; to maintain the necessary conditions of academic freedom.[25]

One writer discusses the "cluster of roles" which the president undertakes: the administrative roles are operational in nature; the promotional roles are cultural, financial, and communicative; and the academic or educational roles include faculty leadership and attention to the philosophy and scholarship of the college.[26]

In whatever arrangement or classification the responsibilities of the college president are reported, they emphasize the fact that his job is one of human relations.

The president and the administrative and teaching faculties. The college president will find that even though he makes policy recommendations to the board of control and even though he is largely responsible for interpreting the board's decisions to the faculty and students, his ideas will be only as good as others believe them to be. The members of the administrative and teaching faculty are the ones who carry out the projects, and it will take a great deal of time for the new president to develop effective relationships with his campus colleagues.

At the outset the president must devise a *modus operandi* and a set of objectives for fulfilling the assigned responsibility. Deciding on the administrative policy of the college is largely the task of the president with the counsel of such administrative assistants as he has.

---

[24] Cowley, *op. cit.*, p. 7.
[25] Stoke, *op. cit.*, pp. 106-7.
[26] Stephens, *op. cit.*, p. 15.

Having accomplished this first mission, he immediately begins building the executive team. The president who is privileged to hire a number of his close associates will discover that a wide circulation of the descriptions of positions to be filled will usually bring a flood of applications.

It is good practice to canvass the college community before circulating information of vacancies off-campus. The right person may be among the college personnel. If this person is found and is interested, a great recruiting ordeal is avoided. Frequently a search both on and off the campus is necessary. Some have found it helpful to send the announcement of the vacancy to a selected list of the most likely sources. It is very important to have clearly in mind the personality, preparation, and talents essential for the position itself and for the team which is being created. It is also important to emphasize the minimal qualifications. If this technique is not successful, then a wider circulation is necessary. If one of two candidates of equal strength is on the campus already, it is important to morale to select the on-campus person.

Few presidents have succeeded in matching the achievement of President Gilman when he assembled the original staff at Johns Hopkins.

> . . . he traveled through America and Western Europe in order to confer with outstanding scholars and scientists of the world before making an important appointment. Specialists in this or that branch may indeed possess the requisite skill and objectivity, but Gilman wished to make certain, and he made certain by going far from Baltimore in order not to be swayed by local or personal considerations. Having chosen his key men, he let them absolutely alone.[27]

Presidents at colleges growing at a modest rate may be permitted to follow the practice of Dr. Gilman, but today's rapidly growing colleges must have many people working at recruitment. Department chairmen, deans, and faculty members—all are sources of suggestions. Recruitment is a demanding responsibility, and the task must be done systematically. In the accelerated hiring needs of many colleges, the president's primary function is to pass judgment on personal qualifications—to decide whether the candidate will work

---

[27] Abraham Flexner, *I Remember* (New York: Simon and Schuster, 1940), p. 48.

effectively and happily within the scope of the mission of the college, and to bring about such balance of interests and points of view as he can among instructors in each discipline.

A concise yet complete job and personal description is prepared for each vacancy and copies are sent to major training institutions and placement offices. At the same time, people on campus who know heads of departments in other colleges and universities inform them of vacancies in their subject area. Direct solicitation of qualified candidates who already hold an appointment at another college is highly questionable.

Recruitment of faculty can be a highly technical process as heads of placement services will corroborate.[28] Some presidents have used suggestions that have come to them from placement service directors and have occasionally received excellent counsel from highly successful colleagues from other campuses. Since recruitment usually takes place over a wide geographical area, it has been found helpful to supply a copy of the college catalog, a view book to give the prospect a feeling of the campus, its facilities, and its people, and information statements from the Chamber of Commerce or similar agency describing the community and its resources. These materials are shared directly with the applicant.

The personal interview should take place after papers and recommendations are received, screened, and put in order of rank. Preferably the most likely persons should be interviewed in two places—on the person's own campus or place of business and on the campus of the college doing the hiring. The most likely candidates should be acceptable to the department (represented by the department or division chairman), the dean of the college, and the president.

When the right person is found, he should be offered the position immediately and—if possible—committed to a decision within a reasonably short time. If he refuses, then the person next preferred should be offered the job. If the first two or three persons on the list do not accept, then it may be wise to recirculate information on the vacancy. Unless the need is very pressing, it will be wise to hold a

---

[28] See, for example, Lloyd D. Bernard, "Placement: Methods used by individuals in finding jobs; methods employed by colleges in securing teachers," *Current Issues in Higher Education, 1956,* edited by G. Kerry Smith (Washington, D.C.: Association for Higher Education, 1956), pp. 138-44.

position open for a year rather than appoint a person who does not seem suitable.

Once employed and properly oriented, the new faculty member begins qualifying for retention and promotion. The requirements for both should be formalized and clearly defined. The retention plan should provide for periodic evaluations of performance, achievement, and growth, and should principally serve as a means of assisting the newcomer to adjust to the campus and fulfill his responsibility.

It is highly important that assessments be made by experienced colleagues, preferably those in the person's teaching and research specialty, and that they be made frequently. Casual and unsolicited comments of students, informal interviews with the person, staff meetings, and observations on preparation of assignments and examinations provide bits of information that can be helpful. If class visits are part of the procedure, the observations made should be discussed immediately following the visit.

Class visits are a highly controversial practice. The quite distinctly opposed schools of thought on this subject are well illustrated by President Emeritus Henry Wriston and President Peter Sammartino, of Fairleigh Dickinson University. The latter holds that "There should be frequent observations of new instructors and less frequent ones of older members of the faculty as a regular part of the administrative procedures within a college. These observations should be made by at least three different persons, probably the head of department, the dean, and the president." Wriston, however, makes a no less unequivocal reference to "an academic tradition stronger than law [that] forbids the president to invade the classroom or tamper directly with instruction. . . ." [29] When classroom observations are to be made, the new appointee ought to be told in advance.

Informal conversations and formal conferences with all new faculty members should be held by the department chairman and, if possible, by the dean to provide them with constructive suggestions and progress reports based on the evaluation procedures. A record of such interviews should be kept by the chairman or the dean with the full knowledge of the faculty member. If all efforts fail, the instructor should be notified at the earilest reasonable time that it is

---

[29] Peter Sammartino, *The President of a Small College* (Rutherford, N. J.: Fairleigh Dickinson College Press, 1954), p. 53; and Wriston, *op. cit.*, p. 132.

unlikely that he will be retained. If the recruitment procedure is effective, this problem should arise rarely. Letting a staff member go is one of a president's most disagreeable responsibilities; when it really is necessary, however, there should be no vacillation or lack of courage.

The plans and procedures in all personnel relations require the president's special attention. It is he who has the ultimate responsibility to see that the techniques or objectives are fair and that they are understood by all concerned.

Most colleges require that there be a probationary period for faculty and although the specific provisions vary, the end result is that once the faculty member has passed through the probationary status, he achieves relatively permanent tenure. It is important that the trial period be sufficiently long to relieve the new faculty member of immediate anxiety and provide an adequate evaluation, yet it should also have some terminal date. A practice of limiting tenure to associate professors and higher levels may not serve in times of critical shortages of teaching faculty. If a teacher serves well over a period of years and makes a sufficient contribution to the life of the campus and the aims of the college, he should be granted tenure privileges even though he may not meet all the criteria for promotion.

Promotion of teaching faculty is a most involved action. Much of what takes place in determining eligibility for retention applies to promotion, and for probationary staff members the two procedures are inseparable. Teaching success, along with research and publication, are normally the primary criteria for promotion. Since teaching success is difficult to measure with any precision, the emphasis tends to fall on research and publication. Although the college may be one which emphasizes research, it is not usually as major a factor as it might be in a university. Because of the special emphasis on teaching and because of the complexity of the promotion process, the president bears an important responsibility. Successful teaching should be a major factor, if not the dominant one, in determining promotion, and the president—whose primary concern is with the total college—must be greatly involved in formulating the criteria and procedures for promotion. He can work successfully with the faculty in setting forth the aims of the college; he can analyze and interpret the resources of the campus and project and chart the growth of the institution. With detailed information, he and the faculty or elected representatives of the faculty can prepare specific guidelines to be followed in the selection process.

Criteria of good teaching and their identification are essential. Weighing of other factors, such as research, publication, and service to community and college, is also necessary. Then a clear statement must be formulated with respect to the roles which each agency of the college may play in the promotion plan.

During all of the procedures for recruitment, hiring, retention, and promotion, the president must be ever mindful of the mission of his college and the important place that all the personnel actions have in the success of the total college community in achieving its aims and objectives.

Unless the college is going to be one which sprints ahead periodically and occasionally limps behind, it must have a balance of age, point of view, and experience among its teaching personnel. Of these factors which must be equated, perhaps the one referred to as "point of view" is the one most difficult to judge yet most important to the welfare of the college. Ordway Tead suggests that faculty philosophies tend to follow one of four classifications about human values. There is *moral nihilism* which is a conscious neutrality or a flat denial of the "reality of life's values." There is *scientism* that finds scientific determinism and materialism to be the sufficient, or only possible, answer. Then there is *scientific humanism,* a presently popular view that contends "The world is man-centered and man natively is sufficiently virtuous to save himself." [30] And lastly there is the traditional theological Christian position. In considering this classification of points of view, most, if not all, colleges would consider themselves more properly "in balance" with very few, if any, moral nihilists!

Other differences of points of view are identifiable and common on college campuses. The excitement of learning is enhanced through meeting a variety of convictions and ideas in the classroom. It is the president's job to see to it that students have this maturing experience.

None of the subject areas should be allowed to lag behind the others in strength. Strong departments keep strong by attracting

---

[30] Ordway Tead, *Trustees, Teachers, Students, Their Role in Higher Education* (Salt Lake City, Utah: University òf Utah Press, 1951), p. 58.

good people and, similarly, comparatively weak ones tend to per-petuate their condition by being able to attract only less well qualified people. Certainly no president wants to hold back any de-partment in order to maintain balance; he always pushes the strong ones forward. What he needs to do is pay special attention to the progressive development of the less successful department. Some-times a change of departmental leadership and realistic assessment are needed to begin the hard climb to respectability. The president must bring weak departments up to the level of superior ones, and he needs to win the support of the board of control and faculty leaders if he is to be successful.

The president's working relationships with the faculty and with the students are very important and interrelated. Although his rela-tionships with the students are usually less direct than with the faculty, the responsibility is no less great.

The president and student welfare. Among the most pleasant and rewarding experiences the president has is his association with student leaders. Most of his meetings with student groups are at formal affairs—assemblies, luncheons, dinners, and forums. Occa-sionally he may have informal visits with the leaders of these student groups. At times he may have opportunities to teach in nonclass-room associations with students; in the process, however, he will find that patience and situational advantages are very important. Keeping a finger on the pulse of student opinion is very important and requires a judicious sifting of fact from fiction.

Student leaders are not unlike leaders in any other environment. They may be less adroit but they are not less aggressive, less im-pulsive, or less committed to cause. Their idealism is sometimes tarnished by some undesirable political conniving, but usually the ideals prevail. Student leaders are proud of their college and wish to have a part in its successes. Frequently they measure up to major responsibilities. Blessed is the college president who has both a rea-sonable and able student body president with whom to work.

The field of student personnel administration has become highly professionalized within the last two decades. The colleges have coped with this increased emphasis on meeting student personal and educational problems in a variety of ways. Some have moved toward highly centralized plans for administering to the student needs. Most commonly the officer in charge of this function is a dean of students, occasionally he is a vice-president in charge of student affairs. Under the aegis of such a person may be included admissions, records, counseling in its various commitments, discipline, co-curricular activities, housing, placement, health services, and student government.

With the increasing size of college enrollments, special professional abilities have been needed to diagnose and treat the various needs of students. The close intimate contact of the teaching and administrative faculty with students that once was possible on the small campus has had to give way to this more professional approach. The president's responsibility in this expanding personnel function is one of planning and evaluation. Within the resources of his institution, he should provide a student personnel program that will augment and enhance the instructional program. In attending to this responsibility, he needs the collaboration of the most able and devoted psychologically-oriented administrators of student personnel that he can find.

In the decades ahead, the problems and challenges in the student personnel area will achieve a complexity perhaps even greater than those in the instructional area. Proper development and management of student publications, residence halls, health services, and social and intellectual affairs will require the most diligent and active participation of the president.

The president and public relations. The president's relations with off-campus groups are as important as those he has with his campus associates. In general, they involve the college's relationships with its alumni, its community, and its off-campus services and are frequently referred to as "public relations." The term *public relations* may be variously defined and probably any definition would lead to some disagreement. Certain authorities believe public relations is the effort of the institution to adapt itself to its social and political environment and to interpret itself to the society of which it is a part. Other authorities suggest the term is a generic one, descriptive of a new kind of social and political engineering.[31] All authorities tend to agree that the conception of public relations as a distinct management activity has emerged within the last three decades.

---

[31] Marvin M. Black, "Some Thoughts on Public Relations Concept," *Pride,* no vol. number (Jan., 1960), p. 12.

Definitions of the president's public relations responsibility are usually broad. As the concept of public relations is broadly or narrowly conceived by the president of the college, so will the program undertaken in this area be narrow or broad in aim and design.

All colleges have some plan of interpreting the purposes and mission of their program to the public. The course of study, the services, and the other facets of the college program are essentially public in character. Indeed, informing the public of the goals and achievements of the college is not a question of privilege, but of obligation. The college receives money, cooperation, interest, and attention from the public. It would be logical, therefore, to conclude that the institution has a duty to give an account of itself periodically.

It is apparent that the colleges of America have recognized their increasing responsibilities in this regard. One index of this fact is the steady growth of the American College Public Relations Association. In 1925 the Association had a membership of 100; in 1940 the number had increased to 554; and in 1960 there were 856 institutional and 1,642 individual members. Figures for the next year reveal an institutional membership over 900, with individual memberships more than double that number.[32] Another indication of increased awareness of responsibility is the changing designation of this association. Originally it was called simply the American Association of College News Bureaus; in 1930 it was renamed American College Publicity Association; and in 1946 the name was changed to American College Public Relations Association, indicating a greater awareness of the need to cultivate a favorable public understanding.

Although public relations is everybody's responsibility in the collegiate institution—administration, faculty, trustees, students, and nonacademic personnel—the president is the key person. On his leadership rests a large part of the burden of building a proper background and basis of public understanding. Any neglect of this responsibility by the president will affect every aspect of the public relations program.

Although the president is a key person in this effort, he need not conduct the public relations program himself. As a matter of fact,

---

[32] *The American College Public Relations Association Newsletter,* Vol. I, No. 1 (Sept., 1961), p. 4.

this would be most unwise, since he usually does not have the time and/or the special skills which the public relations program requires. Therefore he must delegate a major portion of this responsibility to a member of the administrative faculty who will work closely with him. This official needs an intimate knowledge of day to day campus activities in order to assist the president in keeping aware of what is taking place on and off campus.

The title given to the person whom the president selects to handle the public relations responsibility varies widely from one institution to another. According to one survey of colleges, eleven had the title of *Director of Public Relations,* seven were called *Director of University Relations,* four had the title of *Vice-President,* while four adopted *Director of Public Information.* Others used were: *Director of Information, Director of Development, Assistant to the President, Director of Public Services, Director of Information Services,* and *Director of Alumni and Public Relations.*[33]

It is important to choose the title deliberately, because it should give a true picture of the person's actual duties. Under any circumstances, it must be identified with the office of the president in order to give it prestige among the various constituents of the college community. Whether or not the occupant of the public relations post is a member of the teaching faculty depends upon the nature of the institution and the qualifications required for the job. In all cases, it is important that the public relations person have status in the administrative circle of the college. He needs to have access to the sources of information and access to the media through which the information is disseminated.

The late Dr. R. A. Kent of the University of Louisville set out five principles for the relationship between the president and the public relations director:

1. Matters of public relations should be centralized under the administration of a director of public relations.
2. The director of public relations should have a close official connection with the president—in our case he is the Assistant to the President.
3. He should be given aid sufficient to allow him ample time for planning the broad phases of public relations.

---

[33] Victor J. Danilov, "Public Relations Practices at State Universities and Land Grant Colleges," *Pride* (Sept., 1960), pp. 8-14.

4. His salary should be ample to attract and hold a man who has desirable personal traits as well as academic training.
5. He should be the confidential adviser to the president on matters of policy which may result in favorable or unfavorable attitudes on the part of the constituency of the institution.[34]

In delegating the overall coordination of the public relations program to a director, the president should not assume that this is a one-man job. In some institutions an advisory committee in public relations has proved very helpful. Whether the membership on this advisory committee should be limited exclusively to the campus is a matter which can be determined on the basis of the special needs of the institution. A committee may serve a coordinating function and may be of great help in enlisting the support of all the segments of the college community.

In addition to the director of public relations, there are other persons close to the president, besides his official professional staff, who have important roles to play in the public relations responsibility. One of the important persons is the president's secretary. She can gain respect for the president's office and give it an aura of high efficiency. To a considerable extent it is she who determines who will see the college head. She reroutes inquiries and personal visitors coming directly to the office of the president when more helpful attention can be found in one of the other campus offices. The manner in which this routing of visitors is done is an important factor in the campus public relations efforts.

The long-term presidential secretary tends to fit one of several categories. She may be the type who becomes a significant part of the president's office and tends to blend with the total concept of the presidential image; she may be maternal about her duties and her office; or she may be one who has over the years accumulated information and made decisions of an increasingly significant nature to the point that she and her services appear to be indispensable. In whatever category she fits, the president's secretary has a most important place in the presidential office.

Another person who contributes materially to the picture most

[34] Quoted by Waldo E. Reck, *Public Relations, a Program for Colleges and Universities* (New York: Harper & Brothers, 1946), pp. 35-6 from R. A. Kent, "The President and his Publicity Director," *College Publicity Digest* (Feb.-Mar., 1937), p. 4.

people have of the president and his office is the president's wife. Whether consciously or unconsciously, she becomes a part of the presidential image. Observation of the wives of presidents over a number of years leads to the conclusion that the vast majority fall into four principal categories. There are those who deliberately work at the role of being the president's wife. Even though they may possess strong leadership qualities themselves and perhaps even have impelling drives to excel, they have channeled these proclivities into activities which tend to supplement and enhance their husbands' positions.

The second category includes the gracious ladies who are part of the background of the president's existence and yet who feature prominently in the minds of the people who come into contact with the president. These wives apparently do not deliberately work at their role but are unselfishly bent toward making their husband's job as easy as possible by assuming complete responsibility for the activities and affairs that center about the president's home, the children, the home management problems, and the entertainment responsibilities.

A third category of presidents' wives would include those who are strictly homemakers, who shun public notice as much as possible. They seem to be under duress when playing the role of the president's wife and prefer to limit their campus and off-campus associates to a few intimate friends. Such wives have a great desire for anonymity and want no part of the public spotlight.

The fourth group is comprised of those wives who are determined to be disassociated as much as possible from the college and college affairs. To the campus community they appear to be antisocial, but often they are merely fearful of the social activities in which the president must participate. These wives seldom appear, even missing occasions which other presidents' wives regard as command performances. They resent the responsibilities which the office imposes upon them and the limitations it imposes on their husbands.

The president and his leadership responsibility. The president of the college, unlike the manager of a large business or industry, works with experts who have diverse interests in a wide range of fields. His position, in the competitive jargon, is one of pacemaker in the hilltop ivy league, and if he is to be successful in his leadership role, he must ingeniously tap the resources of his own campus. He can expect that the scholars with whom he is associated have wisdom, experience, and a great deal of information that will bear upon the management practices of the college. The president must make use of this reservoir of talent. To utilize best the campus resources the president must recognize the special interests and occasionally even the prejudices of his informed advisers and consultants.

The leadership responsibility of the president requires that he always keep in mind the total instructional program of the college. He strives for a balance of interests and offerings. He sustains institutional standards and encourages development of better ones. He works continuously at the improvement and refinement of techniques of evaluating instruction. He must encourage research and curriculum planning as well as promote efficiency. He must be receptive to new ideas and new techniques, especially new measurement devices.

Inevitably the president will be less expert in certain areas than many of his on-campus colleagues. Nonetheless, any situation involving so many management skills demands leadership, and surely it is the president who must measure up to the major leadership role. As John Gardner has said:

> If one is concerned to bring into the leadership ranks of a profession or a class or a society the men best qualified to exercise that leadership, the sensible thing is to guard the door with rigorous selection procedures, rigorous procedures for testing ability, rigorous courses of preparation. And the purpose of the rigor is not simply to screen out the *less able* but to screen out the *less highly motivated*. The ones who get through will then be not only men of superior ability but men of superior character. The very fact of their surmounting difficult obstacles will have accomplished a vitally important sorting out.[35]

The president, like his political counterparts in municipal, state, and federal government, is increasingly responsible for probing into and defining the objectives of his organization. In this process, he frequently initiates policy.[36]

The faculty becomes the sounding board, the inquisitors, the con-

---

[35] John W. Gardner, *Excellence, Can We Be Equal and Excellent Too?* (New York: Harper & Brothers, 1961), p. 100.

[36] W. H. Cowley suggests that a president should not be a doer, but rather an organizer, planner, and philosopher for the organization; *op. cit.*, pp. 13-14.

sultants, the modifiers, and maybe even the mediators. It is the president's job to ascertain whether the curriculum of the college is meeting the needs of the students and, in the larger sense, the needs of the society the college serves. Is the curriculum a carefully shaped program which will effectively prepare young people for the future? Or is it merely the patched-up result of many faculty quarrels, made up of courses of varying degrees of obsolescence? Are the techniques of teaching keeping pace with the demands of the change in social relationships? Are the members of the college community as critical of the results as they should be? Is the college really interested in bringing out the best in every student it admits, or is it satisfying its institutional ego by a high attrition rate?

The president is not in a position to answer these questions alone.

> He must ask them of the faculty, insistently if he wishes, but with substantial willingness to consider their answers. Faculty members will teach effectively only what they believe in, and not what a president tells them they should teach. His skill as an educational leader lies in uniting them in their views as to the kind of institution they will serve, why it exists at all, for whom it is trying to provide education, and what kind of education it is trying to provide. If these basic ideas are clear, if they are shared by president and faculty, if they are kept bright and resolute through constant examination and discussion, they will do more to ease the strains and release the energies of the institution than will any number of new millions in endowment.[37]

After twenty-eight years as a college president, Donovan was of the opinion that a president "can render his best service on the campus, working with faculty and students. It is not good for his college for him to be a suitcase president." President Donovan suggests that perhaps there might be another officer known as the "traveler." Hadley of Yale appointed Anson Phelps Stokes as Secretary of Yale which meant he served as the president's *alter ego,* and could travel for him.[38]

The president needs to work closely with student organizations and student leaders in making clear to them and to all the students the essential purpose of the college. In the president's messages, in such publications as the student handbooks, yearbooks, and campus

---

[37] Stoke, *op. cit.,* pp. 127-28.
[38] Herman L. Donovan, "The Changing Conception of the College Presidency," *Association of American Colleges Bulletin* (March, 1957), pp. 44-5.

news media, the president can impress on the students the importance of the instructional program and their own part in making it a valuable experience for themselves.

The president should remind the students periodically of the role of the faculty, the intent of the course of study, and the intellectual nature of the college. His remarks may support other services of the college to inspire the students to do their very best.

A part of the learning process is the achievement of an understanding of responsible behavior. Students need to know that an educated person should not casually offer random criticism and that constructive criticism is justified by the beneficial results it can achieve. The president, whose ear is so persistently sought, must make it clear that to initiate or circulate unfounded accusations and criticisms is dishonorable. The college campus is not a place for small minds and unbridled freedom. The pursuit of knowledge is a rigorous one and requires sustained discipline. The students learn their lessons best if frequently reminded of the level of maturation it is assumed they have attained when they enroll in college.

With the faculty, the president's leadership effort is less overt. He does not maintain a position, he arranges a climate. His objective is a continuous sustaining effort to excel; he needs to succeed in giving this effort direction and organization. The president encourages the faculty to take an active part in the management of the college and yet at the same time frees them to attend to the primary business of instruction. He breeds confidence in their abilities to do well the assignments they bear and keeps the classroom the domain of the teacher.

President Wriston of Brown maintains that though the president cannot interfere in classroom instruction, he can have a great deal to do with other educational aspects of college life. Three very important areas are the library, the dormitories, and the grounds.[39] The intelligent and proper development of the physical plant is a major responsibility of the president of the college. He determines the needs, programs the facilities, and initiates and sustains the long-range plan which is essential if the obligation of the college for its expanding enrollment is to be met. The job of the president increasingly requires special knowledge and skills. At the same time

[39] Wriston, *op. cit.*, pp. 132-51.

he must have the prophet's ability to visualize each stage of the program before it unfolds.

He is the leader, and leadership will soon bare the soul of any man. It is no place for the timid or the novice. It will reward the few of noble natures and best accommodate those who have learned their boxing lessons well—to roll with the punches.

The leadership factor is the thread which ties the college together. The manner in which it is interwoven in the woof and warp of the college will determine to a very great extent the success of the administrator.

The president seemingly has great power. He may use it sparingly or generously. In a frantic effort to perform his almost impossible job, he may incline toward dictatorial tactics; he may even yield to the temptation to become a ruthless head knocker.

What then are the restraining influences? What forces keep the president attentive to the best interests of his campus? Essentially the president must earn the respect and loyalty of his associates. His leadership role is a continuous one—with the students, with the administrative and teaching faculty, with the nonprofessional staff and community leaders. He is always an opinion maker and a pace setter. His personal qualities are his most effective assets. One observer declared in his discussion of presidential associations that no president can retain effective relations with his faculty if they lose faith in his personal honesty and integrity.[40] This same qualification can be made of the president's leadership role in all of his associations. The quality of character is the most influential factor in the president's professional life.

---

[40] Stephens, *op. cit.*, p. 146.

CHAPTER III

Leadership in Decision Making

Working with Administrative Faculty

It is in dealing with people that the most difficult decisions must be made. Top executives of large businesses contend that problems of finance, marketing, product design, and sales techniques have solutions that come with almost mathematical certainty if painstaking study, orderly research, and experiential knowledge are brought to bear; but it is the solution to problems of the people with whom they work which eludes them and causes them loss of sleep.

Although college administration markedly differs from industrial management, the most worrisome problems involved in decisions about people are present to even a greater extent. The president of the college has administrative colleagues to whom are delegated large measures of authority in appointing, promoting, and retaining staff members. In every facet of personnel management, decisions are made which influence the growth and development of the college as well as its people. The actions taken are often legally correct, but are the moral obligations to both the people and the college clearly met?

To lessen the number of mistakes in personnel transactions, it is important—even necessary—to have a continuous in-service personnel management program for administrative faculty. Department chairmen, associate deans, and deans (and yes, presidents) can profit from workshops and seminars devoted at least partially to better management. Personnel relations, especially, are never so expertly handled that improvement is not possible. Handbooks and other guides which outline procedures may be helpful, but there is no substitute for the preparation of all persons in decision-making responsibilities involving fellow staff members. Extensive planning in advance can make such decision-making relatively simple. The responsibility for instituting this program lies with the president.

He may initiate the preparation of an administrative manual

which includes specific instructions to department chairmen and deans in the techniques for managing personnel procedures. Periodically he may devote meetings of the administrative faculty to discussions of good practice in personnel administration.

It is well for the president to remember that his seemingly powerful decision-making authority is only as secure as the competency and loyalty of his administrative aids. Therefore the careful selection and in-service preparation of administrative faculty is of very great importance to proper institutional management.

To the president who is free to choose a number of his assistants, the test is one of introspection. What are his personal strengths and shortcomings? He must face his qualities objectively and honestly, because an accurate assessment is necessary if he is to bring in associates who will form a successful team.

If the president's analysis of his assets and deficiencies reveals important areas where supplemental strengths are required, then his first appointments should be made to fill these needs. Even the more glamorous roles may need to be delegated if the president knows another person can be more successful in them than he. Once the position has been defined and filled, the president must give his support unstintingly. Confidence and trust from above encourage loyalty and dedication.

In many situations, if not most, the president "inherits" his administrative staff. The new football coach is given a comparatively free hand in naming his associates. The dean frequently is privileged to name his aids, since the dean's principal helpers are usually active members of the instructional faculty who prefer to return to teaching when the new dean is named. But the president cannot ordinarily expect the deans to return voluntarily to teaching; it is not likely in many cases that the deans have kept abreast of their disciplines. And they may not be privileged to exercise this option even if they so desired.

The new president under these circumstances has two diagnostic jobs—he tabulates his own debits and credits and does his best similarly to analyze his administrative faculty. If it is not clear to the president when he first comes into his post what the relative strengths and shortcomings of his administrative staff are, a series of staff meetings will soon identify the special gifts of each of his principal colleagues.

It is probably just as well to seek the aid of assistants closest to him in responsibility and authority in this second analysis, and he should not be too surprised to get more assistance than he bargains for. The president may receive candid and perceptive help from his subordinates if he asks them to present their own interests and abilities. This kind of analysis is a continuous one for the president of the college. "Developing his own team constitutes no adverse judgment of the previous administration. The group surrounding the president must fit his rhythm." [1]

When the audit has been made, then the team concept should evolve. The directional influence emanates from the president. He organizes the personal resources of his team; he follows up assignments; he inspires, exhorts, and requires; he practices the preaching of Emerson, "There is no limit to what can be accomplished if it doesn't matter who gets the credit."

In a small college the staff meetings may be infrequent, but the personal face-to-face meeting between the president and individual deans and other administrative personnel may be numerous. Such relationships strengthen the effectiveness of the team and build morale. All have a stake in the success or failure of projects. In a large college more formal techniques are necessary. Administrative faculty meetings will be required on a regular schedule. Since these are work conferences, agenda, minutes, and procedural patterns are important. The essential factor in either the informal small college situation or the more formal large college plan is that all information relevant to the resolution of a problem be shared with team members.

There is a place on the administrative faculty for numerous talents that are important in the success of the operational function. The confidant of the faculty will be blessed with great tenderness and compassion, for the personnel problems in any institution are many. The expediter will need a generous supply of cool, calculating analytical ability. Suspended judgment on problems of great concern is essential in the patient planner, for time is required to uncover relevant information and to provide a transition period from a temporary state of panic to one of calm reflection. The ad-

---

[1] Wriston, *op. cit.*, p. 152.

ministrative staff also must have a sensitivity to the unexpressed needs of the faculty and the students.

To make the best use of administrative talents, it is important to have a clear definition of the individual responsibilities of the administrative faculty. A clear delegation of authority commensurate with responsibility is essential. This can be accomplished through a job analysis procedure and a description which is made part of an administrative manual. To supplement the job descriptions there needs to be also an outline of the procedures which may be most effective in given situations. The president himself must be quite sure not to short-circuit his administrative faculty by requesting or permitting one of his aids to assume responsibilities clearly within the province of another of his associates. Periodic staff meetings serve as an important regulatory device. At such meetings all persons present may be kept informed concerning the major activities of each person on the administrative team. Furthermore, staff meetings enable an administrative head to gain helpful information from others of his associates who may have had experience and responsibility with the problem while each benefits from the opportunity to express himself on matters of mutual interest and concern.

President Wriston suggested another approach, however. He strongly emphasized the point that administrators have to be kept actively interested, and this influenced his whole concept of organization:

> . . . in policy-making posts particularly—appointing good people is only half the battle—or even less. Keeping them interested and refreshing their viewpoints are just as important. I believe the key to that is the same as with the president himself. They must be provided with variety in their work, lest routine sap all the liveliness from their tasks. Administration calls for endless repetition— but not necessarily by the same person all the time. For this reason I developed a theory of administration which I cannot claim was ever popular; indeed my associates sometimes complained of it rather bitterly. However, it was based on conviction and experience.
>
> To state it is simple: I never had a chart of organization or a set of sharply prescribed duties. If an officer worked out such a scheme it was subject to change—on short notice. On one occasion at Brown I asked two vice-presidents virtually to exchange duties. This was not because I was dissatisfied with either; both had performed admirably. But I thought further continuance of established patterns would soon lead to their being frozen. The exchange was

salutary. Both continued to do admirably; neither handled his new assignments just as his predecessor had; each got a fresh perspective on old and familiar problems.[2]

At the beginning of each year it is well for the president, with the help of his administrative associates, to chart the course of the institution. This effort aims at the most significant accomplishment which should be reached during the ensuing twelve months. A general conference should be followed by individual conferences with principal subordinates. In each case, specific objectives are listed for the subordinate in keeping with the common objectives agreed upon at the planning meeting of the staff. A record of these conferences is made for both the president and the assistant. Changes in this prospectus may be made during the course of the weeks and months to follow, but at the end of the year the president should have another conference to see how much has been achieved. This technique has many advantages over the practice of making annual reports because face-to-face discussions of the important projects and effectuations can be significant aids in the long-range charting of the course of the college. In a growing institution the long-range vision is abetted by detailed day-to-day planning. The table of organization is modified, refinements of job descriptions evolve, more effective channels of communications develop, shortcomings and potential abilities are discovered. Each day should have some time set aside for reflection on these important considerations in the administrative process.

A responsibility which plagues the administrator working with several communities is the organization of his own time. Unless his time be well organized, that of his subordinates may well be dissipated. Therefore it is incumbent on both the person and those about him to have a pattern which they may follow in conducting the business of the institution.

Each day should be separated into time blocks, at least for the important responsibilities the office entails. The schedule will vary according to the person and the order of importance which he gives to the various items of business. Many prefer to do the paper work and planning during the early part of the day, leaving the remainder of the day free for personal visits, community contacts, and prob-

---

[2] *Ibid.,* pp. 155-56.

lems that take up varying amounts of time. Planning the day in this particular manner is helpful also to the secretarial staff.

Working with the Trustees

A college president's success is measured in terms of his educational leadership; he should not be a mere sycophant of the trustees. It is vital, nevertheless, that he have a good relationship with the board of control. The board selects him and, in case of serious differences, the board releases him. Unfortunately, there is considerable difference of opinion on the part the board should play in the management of the college, even though its legal authority is clear. Trustees, college presidents, and members of the teaching faculty look upon the functions of the trustees from points of view that reflect their own preconceptions and experience. Trustees have often expressed differing conceptions of their responsibilities. Teaching and administrative faculties and some presidents too tend to define the board's role so as to eliminate its interference, but here again no group has a single conception of the job of the board. On occasion, the difference of opinion relative to the function of the trustees is more in degree than in kind.[3]

In at least one area there is little disagreement about the responsibility which the board of trustees bears. The trustees are expected to provide the resources necessary to support adequate salaries and to furnish the essential facilities including the equipment required for a quality program.[4]

In working with the board of trustees the president is ever conscious of his responsibility to assist them to understand and appreciate the educational program and the needs of the institution.[5] He is responsible for the two-way communication between the campus communities and the board, and in the process he needs to emphasize the special responsibilities expected of the agencies whose ac-

---

[3] For a comprehensive treatment of the functions of boards of trustees, the reader is referred to the volume on this subject in *The Library of Education* series.

[4] Corson, *op. cit.*, pp. 54-5.

[5] An excellent discussion of this responsibility may be found in Beardsley Ruml and Donald H. Morrison, *Memo to a College Trustee, a Report on Financial and Structural Problems of the Liberal College* (New York: McGraw-Hill Book Company, Inc., 1959), Part 5, "The Informed Trustee, A Major Responsibility of the President," pp. 77-94.

tivities he correlates. Faculty members recognize that the board has ultimate decision-making authority; however, they may properly expect the board to allow adequate opportunity for the expression of considered faculty opinion. Trustees in general have a greater concern with the objectives and direction of the college program than with the details of the college operation. Therefore the president has to be a skillful blender of differing points of view which will result in decisions being respected by all agencies affected.

The president must create an awareness on the part of the trustees of the purposes for which the institution was created and for which it draws its financial support. To create this understanding it will be necessary to analyze and determine the implications of the charter, articles of incorporation, public statements, minutes of sponsoring bodies, legislation (in the case of public institutions), and official documents, all of which may pertain to a clarification of the objectives that give direction to the institution.[6]

The official documents and the record of actions of the trustees and other governing agencies may be considered commitments of a binding nature unless there is evidence of subsequent change of intent through proper legal procedure. A difficulty that will often occur is that the purposes giving direction to the college may be so general as to provide little specific guidance.[7] It becomes necessary in such circumstances for the president and the trustees to interpret explicitly what goals will fulfill the legal or corporate obligation of the institution. To give proper attention to this responsibility, the president will find it necessary to make full use of the members of his administrative staff, the faculty, and the trustees themselves.

Once the aims of the college are quite clear, they may be used as a basis of evaluating the institution's programs and its plans for action; they will serve, too, as a guide for future development. From the faculty and the trustees the president should seek concurrence in, as well as complete understanding of, the aims and the educational program of the institution.

It is most important that the president obtain a clear understand-

---

[6] In this section dealing with boards of control we have especially drawn on "Functions of Boards of Trustees in Higher Education," issued by the Commission on Institutions of Higher Education of the Middle States Association of Colleges and Secondary Schools, Document No. 4.10, Feb., 1957.

[7] *Ibid.*, p. 1.

ing of the relationship of his office to the board of trustees.[8] It should be understood that he is the chief executive officer and that he is the individual through whom the board exercises its authority and control.

It is conceded that the selection of the president is one of the very important responsibilities of the trustees, and it follows quite logically that it is also a major responsibility of the board to evaluate the success of his leadership and if necessary to replace him. Having been chosen, however, the president is responsible for executing the policies of the board and he should expect board support without its interference in the details of college management. A clear analysis of the duties of the board and the responsibilities of the president and of the faculty can result in excellent relationships between the president, the board, and the faculty. These position descriptions will inevitably be the president's responsibility.

The leadership role of the president is probably most subtle and indirect in his relationships with the trustees of the college. The president, as the chief executive officer, may expect to assume certain specific responsibilities that relate to the proper function of the board of control. He must see that the board adopts and codifies rules and regulations which include a description of the duties and responsibilities of its own officers. The president should be designated the chief executive officer and in this capacity should be held accountable for implementing board actions. Furthermore, in this official function he needs to be a member of all board committees.

The president provides for the orderly recording of board minutes, with all actions indexed serially as they are adopted or considered. An annual summary index is of great importance. He should see to it that there is a proper distribution of minutes in order to assure implementation and understanding as required. It is essential that the president arrange the media of communication to convey the considered judgments of the academic community on proposals that affect their interests. It is important that such communications be channeled through the office of the president. In order to increase the trustees' knowledge of the educational program, representatives of the academic community should be invited

---

[8] Fuller statements on this relationship may be found in *Ibid.*, Section II, and *Manual for Boards of Regents, New Mexico State Educational Institutions* (Santa Fe, N. M.: Board of Educational Finance, 1955), pp. 20-34.

to meet periodically with the board and describe projects and needs that merit board attention and require board action.

In order to keep the board conversant with trends and developments as well as with best practice in college administration, it is important that its officers and other members be encouraged to attend conferences and meetings of a regional or national nature. From such meetings and the associations they afford can come important benefits to the trustees themselves and to the colleges they represent. Board members can be increasingly effective if they have opportunities to broaden their understandings of the responsibilities they bear.

When trustees visit the campus it is the president's duty to see that appropriate social amenities are arranged. Certainly the trustees should be present or represented at the college for public ceremonies and major events. It has long been accepted that the trustees can and do play a major role in college public relations. If the president is successful in giving the leadership that is expected of him by the board of trustees, the board will be fully informed and can aid immeasurably in interpreting the college to the patrons, the parents, and potential benefactors. As responsible citizens, members of the board of trustees have affiliations that are of unusual value to the college for its orderly growth and development especially in times of crisis or need.[9]

A major responsibility of the trustees, which requires a considerable amount of attention and leadership on the part of the president, is financial support and expenditure. Although the president should provide leadership for financial policy, it should be clearly understood that the trustees are responsible for raising funds. Public institutions of higher education are dependent to a large measure upon legislative appropriations for their financial resources. In many cases, funds received from the public treasury are supplemented by endowments which require wise investment policies. Both government and private donors are particularly concerned that funds be expended in accordance with established specifications. The president is required to provide through his staff accurate and detailed information with respect to the financial needs of the institution

---

[9] Tead, *op. cit.*, pp. 2, 9; Corson, *op. cit.*, p. 57; Raymond M. Hughes, *A Manual for Trustees of Colleges and Universities*, 3rd ed. (Ames, Iowa: Iowa State College Press, 1951), pp. 83-4; and Comm. on I. of H. Ed., *op. cit.*, p. 4.

and the anticipated sources of revenue, and he must insure a careful accounting of the funds received. Wriston declared:

> Managing to live with a board of trustees is like riding a spirited horse that is very skittish. Trustees will shy at a shadow rather more quickly than at real danger. Nonetheless, people like to ride spirited horses, and after one has learned the art it is a thrilling experience, and never boring.[10]

The college presidency is full of challenges. Certainly one of the most important, that which can also be one of the most rewarding to his college, is the cultivation of the sympathetic support of his board of trustees.

Working with the Teaching Faculty and Faculty Organizations

Authority is delegated by the board of control to the president of the college and then by him to elected or appointed officers and committees of the faculty. There are cases in which boards of trustees have made direct delegation of certain responsibilities in the instructional area to recognized agencies of the faculty. In any case, whether authority is delegated directly from the board or from the president, a document of agreements is essential. This may be a charter, a constitution, or minutes and records of the trustees. The statement of agreements should be simple yet explicit; the nature, the extent and limits of authority in responsibility should be clear.

Usually the formal relationships between the board of control and the college president are delineated in rules and regulations of the board and the contract with the president. The policy determining function is the responsibility of the board of control, and the administrative function is the responsibility of the college president. The change of personnel in all major offices on a college campus is sufficiently frequent to merit a similar understanding between the board, the president, and the faculty. The teaching staff expects to recommend policies in the instructional area and it expects to participate in administrative decisions affecting itself.

Members of a college faculty have highly specialized talents and frequently have quite individual interests. If the faculty is to par-

---

10 Wriston, *op. cit.,* p. 84.

ticipate in activities of an all-college nature, organized effort is essential. An orderly process should be agreed to by the faculty and the president whereby faculty recommendations and observations reach decision-making offices. It is during the group dynamics phase that much future contention and misunderstanding can be resolved. If faculty committees and councils working on policy matters and procedures include those members of the administration most involved or concerned with the subject under study, then both relevant information and understanding can be exchanged. It is important that this association begin at the start of the project. When members of campus groups and agencies meet only among themselves, points of view become set and lines of action become rigid. Too frequently when teaching faculty and administrative faculty meet independently to study a plan or course of action, the reconciliation of differing views requires the painful process of negotiation or even arbitration. Mutual respect and college-wide interests are more likely to develop when potentially conflicting views are resolved in the deliberation phase of the study.

Participation in policy-making is of keen concern to the faculty member and rightfully so. The dedicated teacher has reason to be vitally interested in the policy of the college in which he may spend his professional life. By the time he has established himself in a college, a professor already has a great investment. He has prepared himself carefully and thoroughly for his responsibility, often at great expense of time and money. He has chosen a position that appeals to him and has been selected after presenting references and evidence of personal and professional competence. Although his colleagues theoretically accord him status as "one among peers," it takes a while for him to find his place on campus. After he has gone through this demanding process of preparation and examination, it is natural that he be very much interested in the destiny of his college, and that he should expect to confer and participate in policy matters. Assuredly he gains satisfaction from successful teaching and from the excitement of research and discovery, and he also gets professional satisfaction from knowing that there is a place for faculty views in decision-making affecting its own interests.

The organization through which the faculty best can carry on its deliberations and express itself will vary according to institutional characteristics. Past experience, size of the faculty, relative importance of teaching and research, ratio of full-time to part-time faculty, the number of majors, and many other factors determine the plan most effective for a given college. These are among the special considerations the president must be attentive to in building a working relationship with and among his faculty. If the college is small and destined to grow slowly, the entire teaching and administrative faculty can meet frequently and do much of the institution's business. On campuses which have several hundred faculty members or which have the prospect of growing to such size, it is incumbent on all concerned to develop some kind of representative body to meet periodically. This usually will be called a *senate, council,* or *assembly.* The representative body should include both teaching and administrative faculty and should have constituents from all facets of the college community. It is important that the teaching representatives on this body be elected and that some rotation of membership be provided. All these provisions should be specified in a written charter or constitution agreed to by the faculty and the president.

To deal with specific areas of concern to the college it is most expeditious to follow the time proven practice of establishing a committee system whereby issues can be explored thoroughly before being brought to the parent body. Permanent or standing committees are logical for such matters as curricular changes, academic standards, and student affairs. *Ad hoc* committees may be appointed when the problem or project does not come within the province of a standing committee. If the committees are to perform effectively, they should be genuinely functional. Standing committees should be few in number and should have a defined area of competence.

To insure that committee contributions are useful, it is necessary to include in the membership appropriate faculty talent and interest. A committee on committees is in the best position to exercise a selection process, and it is a device preferable to direct presidential appointment, especially for the study of policy matters. The principle is well established that faculty participation in policy determination is desirable; therefore, the constituency of the committee should be determined largely by faculty election.

It is good practice to provide for at least one presidential appointment on each committee. Even with the thoughtful consideration which the committee on committees may give to balancing representation, the president often can further this aim if he makes his appointment after other members have been selected. Occasionally, also, personal antagonisms may result in the exclusion of an unusually able and highly competent individual; through presidential appointment such a person's contributions can be added to those of other committee members. The president should make it quite clear to his appointees, whether drawn from the administrative or teaching faculty, that they need not consider themselves committed to a special point of view.

Committees occasionally appear to have impelling temptations to drift into administrative duties, although experience suggests that they are not effective in such responsibilities. To keep before the committee its primary responsibility for recommending policy and to keep before the committee an effective orderly process, a manual of procedures can be helpful. The manual may be a separate agreement between the faculty, the president, the board of control, or a part of a larger statement of working relationships. Such a document should spell out the committees' purposes and responsibilities and suggest procedural guidelines. Among the matters to which special attention should be given is an underscoring of the importance of agenda planning.

For committees and for faculty councils or senates, the agenda-making process is one of detailed advance planning. To make maximum effective use of the deliberating body, the issues, the choices suggested—preferable in order of importance and with helpful background information—should be prepared during the agenda-planning process. The meeting time of the total membership of committees, or the senates, or the councils, may be more profitably spent on policy matters. The president has the responsibility to take such precautions as he can to insure the thoughtful and effective functioning of these campus groups. It is far better to spend extra time preparing a presentation than to permit an impulsive action which will require reconsideration later and may result in tensions which need never have developed. Enough surprise ventures and reactions will develop in the carefully planned meeting of faculty members to satisfy the most adventuresome soul.

It is well to be aware that unanimous agreement by academicians is seldom reached, and because there are many issues which require action, time is always limited for any one item on the agenda. As much deliberation as possible should be permitted, however, in order to bring into focus the interplay of limited and highly specialized interests.

When a storm is brewing in the council or senate, it is often discreet to halt the discussion and refer the matter to a competent committee for further study and a report at a subsequent meeting. Insofar as possible, action on a problem should be continuous until it is resolved. Nothing is more frustrating to a faculty than a do-nothing disposition in quarters where decisions should be made.

Unfortunately, it is not likely that the individual faculty member will feel that his views are of much moment in the faculty meeting or the large college senate. After experiencing a number of frustrations in this large deliberative body, he may feel a sense of dismay or even despair. He may be moved to agree with the dean of a college of arts and sciences who exclaimed after an exasperating clash, "The faculty council is the combined imbecility of otherwise individually intelligent men." Or he may see himself sitting and knitting like Madame DeFarge in *Tale of Two Cities* as the guillotine of prolonged debate decapitates another good idea.

Many who have extraordinary talent and patience when teaching or doing research cannot accustom themselves to follow all the highways and byways of a faculty council debate, only to discover there will be no noteworthy conclusion. For them the most satisfying participation often can be gained in gatherings devoted to specific professional issues. The president can tap this resource of interest potential and convert it into a significant advance in institutional integration and morale by encouraging special forums and conferences on topics of college-wide importance.

Maintaining communication between campus groups is vital to vigorous institutional life, and all the means for faculty participation serve this function. There are other techniques, more specifically for contact with individuals, which the president can use and promote. Much is made of the "open door" policy of a number of successful administrators. In theory the president is always available and the judgment of whether his time is properly spent on the issue at hand is the responsibility of the person who seeks the opportunity to sit down and think a matter through. For many members of the college community the assurance that this course is always available is perhaps a comforting one.

Unfortunately, the demanding schedule of the college president necessitates making office appointments. Certain times of the day should be set aside specifically for people who need to talk with the president about their problems and their ideas. The college community, which sees itself as an association of peers, does not lend itself easily to the use of official channels of communication; many matters come directly to the office of the president which may more properly be handled at a lower echelon. Under such circumstances, it is the job of the president tactfully to reroute a person to the appropriate college official.

Exchange of correspondence between the president and his colleagues among the teaching faculty serves to preserve important decisions and understandings in writing. If the agreements, assignments, and commitments are a matter of precedent, then they should certainly be put in writing. On occasion, however, criticisms, accusations, or even invective may come to the president by letter or memorandum. If he yields to impulse he may respond in writing and in kind. Under these circumstances, the counsel once offered by a wise dean is very apropos. He advised:

> . . . never write a letter under strain and duress. Go see the person who causes you pain. Go see him if he is across the hall, across the campus, or across the city or state. What you have to say is more effectively said face to face. What you say by pen or print may not be moderated or mitigated. Like stone, what you write stands hard and permanent.

More frequently than a person sometimes recognizes or admits, nice things are said to and done for him. Such welcome solace is most likely to be remembered with warm feeling if it is acknowledged with a written note of gratitude. For his part, the president can show his thoughtfulness by remembering birthdays and important holidays and other memorable occasions. The faculty like to know the president has consideration for individuals.

Each campus needs an official house organ to disseminate information of general interest as well as special items which will appeal to limited groups. The house organ should originate from an office close to the president's, and should make every effort to keep the campus news pertinent and complete. Everyone on campus should feel free to bring to the attention of the editor of the house organ information he feels is of general interest. The house organ is the means of disseminating the results of senate meetings, major committee recommendations, and other matters that may create a better understanding of the day-to-day activities of the college. If this publication is well done, it will constitute a record that has some historical value for the campus.

No matter how well developed the official channels of communication are, a good deal of the information may filter into the president's office by informal means allied to the ever present source of information called the "grapevine." These informal channels may be the best means the president has for anticipating a problem before it becomes a serious and formidable issue. Discreet inquiries followed by exploratory conferences may head off a tempest that would later require a great deal of time and administrative attention.

The object of all the means of communication with which the president is associated is to keep him informed about what is transpiring on campus and to keep the campus community informed about ideas which he feels he should share.

Two of the officers closest to the president will be the elected representative of the faculty of the college and the president of the student body. These officers should be members of one of the standing committees with which the president meets frequently. Elected officers may be the best intermediaries the president can have with the constitutent membership of the college community.

A contention that there is no difference between administrative and teaching faculty is not likely to pass unchallenged, no matter how conscientiously the president works to eliminate a dichotomy. This does not mean that there is necessarily a great difference of philosophy or goals between teaching and administrative faculty, it is simply that their respective responsibilities tend to foster different orientations.

The teaching faculty member feels closest to colleagues in his own discipline. The hierarchical relationship of his loyalties will be first to his discipline, then to his division (if the division embraces two or more departments), and after that to the college as a whole. It is simply that the problems of college-wide import are more remote from the teaching faculty member than the problems that confront him in his own discipline.

The administrative faculty member may look at the relative importance of loyalties from the other end of the spectrum; that is, he

may be concerned first with the problems of institution-wide signifi-
cance, then with those that have divisional implication, and then,
more remotely with those problems that pertain to a specific discipline or subject area. This difference in orientation doubtless has
been the major cause of the estrangement between teaching and administrative faculty. The president's job is to bring about as much
understanding as he possibly can between the differing points of
view that may arise quite naturally by virtue of this difference in
orientation.

Dr. Wriston points out another comparison between teachers and
administrators which may contribute understandable differences.
The scholar has a passion for working until all the evidence is in
before he makes a decision, and the

> ... difference between scholarship and administration lies precisely
> at that point. The administrator faces deadlines; he must act on
> the evidence available. As a scholar, no one could hurry me; I
> wrestled with problems until I was completely convinced before
> taking a position. As administrator, no such luxury was available;
> there comes a time of decision.[11]

The president must understand that the teaching faculty is composed of scholars, teachers, and researchers who have intense interests. They have the pride and prejudices of highly competent
specialists and, understandably, will jealously guard their specialties.
The idea has been emphasized that teaching and research are the
most important responsibilities of the college and so the president
may find it difficult to achieve the peer status that he would like to
have with his teaching colleagues. He may be puzzled and dismayed
when the faculty does not accord the administrator the same high
status which is given the professor. The reason is that the teaching
faculty simply do not regard administration so important a part of
the college cosmos as teaching and scholarship.

If the president plays his role well, he need have a minimum of
misunderstanding about the importance of his leadership responsibility. Harold Taylor, formerly president of Sarah Lawrence College, described very well the attitude needed by the college president
in working with campus colleagues:

---

[11] *Ibid.,* p. 101.

In making decisions, he is not deciding for himself on the basis of his administrative authority what everyone else must do: he is choosing particular courses of action from the many alternatives which, in the view of his student, faculty, and trustee associates, show most promise of contributing to the total aim of the community. His ability to get things done, in any democratic institution, depends upon the trust which his associates place in him, a trust which either develops or declines on the basis of the daily decisions he makes throughout each year. When he presents a point of view of his own, it must be one which he is prepared to argue in its merits, not as a presidential point of view from which there is no retreat. His best means of achieving the leadership which his college needs is to spend time with his colleagues in the faculty and to give encouragement and practical support to ideas which they develop together.[12]

Even a casual reading of the literature related to faculty participation in decision-making, including statements emanating from professional organizations such as the American Association of University Professors, indicates that a power struggle is well under way among segments of the college community.

The American Association of University Professors has in a number of its statements made direct claim that the authority of college teaching faculties should be increased. The Association contends the teaching faculty should have major control over the educational and research policies of the institution. It is preferable, from the Association's view, that this responsibility legally be placed under faculty control. If this is not possible, it is felt that at least a large share of the responsibility should be theirs.[13] According to the Association's statement, teaching faculty also should be empowered to elect representatives for "meaningful participation in the selection and dismissal of deans, presidents" and other college administrators,[14] and should also have a direct role in making budget decisions at all levels.

In California during the 1961 legislative session, the Association of California State College Professors supported legislation which would make it mandatory for teaching faculty to have representation in academic senates engaged in policy formation both for their

---

[12] Harold Taylor, *On Education and Freedom* (New York: Abelard-Schuman, 1954), p. 70.

[13] AAUP, *op. cit.,* p. 204.

[14] *Ibid.*

individual campuses and for the state-wide system.[15] The Association also supported a bill which would provide a biennial evaluation of the administrative policies and practices of the state colleges by elected faculty representatives. The same bill expressed the intention that the faculty should participate in the selection of administrators at the departmental, divisional, and all college levels.[16]

Professor Max Savelle, of the University of Washington, has offered a hypothetical arrangement to provide good faculty participation in state university government. He would have the faculty elect five members of a governing board of nine. These faculty governors would be responsible to the university senate which in turn would be elected by the full-time tenured faculty. The senate would have full legal authority in all internal matters of the university and would have full power to discuss any issue of university interest with the board of governors. The university's president would be nominated by the senate and under certain circumstances might even override the board of governors' refusal to confirm their choice. The president would be legally responsible to the senate.[17]

Ordway Tead, himself an experienced trustee, wrote that he could foresee that it would become increasingly common to have direct faculty representation on trustee boards. Although recognizing such a development certainly has potentiality for difficulty, Tead believes that it would bring a better relationship between trustees and faculties.[18]

Administrative personnel and specifically several college presidents have candidly voiced their own convictions about the action administrators should take in the struggle for power that is now in evidence.

Francis Horn, president of the University of Rhode Island, advocates that these faculty pressures be resisted. Administrators, he writes, must "unite against the common foe—the faculty!" [19] President Horn's thesis is that through the aggressive efforts of college faculties much of the power and authority of administrators have

---

[15] SR 98, AR 78, California State Legislature, 1961.

[16] AB 2240, California State Legislature, 1961.

[17] Max Savelle, "Democratic Government of the State University: a Proposal," *American Association of University Professors Bulletin,* XLIII, No. 1, Spring 1957, pp. 326-28.

[18] Tead, *op. cit.,* p. 7.

[19] Francis H. Horn, "Academic Administrators, Unite!" *College and University Business,* XXX, No. 12 (June, 1961), p. 33.

fallen away. He contends that the administrators have a responsibility to take the offensive to recover and reëstablish their authority and their power. He observes that administrators of colleges historically have defended the teaching faculty against pressures from the public and the government alike. At times administrators have thus jeopardized their prestige and their jobs. Administrative officers have been working for unity and cohesion with the teaching faculty but, according to President Horn, the teaching faculty has marshaled its resources in opposition to administrators.

President Elbin of West Liberty State College in West Virginia seems to concur in the frequently repeated observation made by a president of a great university that "academic communities, whatever their protestations to the contrary, really prefer anarchy to any form of government." [20] He also voices concern about the current struggle in academic circles. Elbin finds part of the explanation of unrest in the opinion that college faculties are deteriorating in quality each year. A further explanation, he believes, is that faculty members today are extremely security-minded, both with respect to their personal finances and in response to criticism of the profession, which has grown sharp and abrasive.

At least a part of the reason for the power struggle now under way in higher education is that administrators have not been as expert as they should be in making decisions. They have failed to bring into the decision-making process the facilities and techniques commonly available in other areas. They have watched computers unravel great snarls of numerical data to give insight into the resolution of many problems in business and industry. They have seen automatic pilots developed to take the error out of navigating fast flying aircraft, but in their own decision-making techniques they are still flying by the seat of their pants.

It is quite appropriate that the faculty challenge the decision-making procedures of their administrators. Probably administrators are still relying on experience and intuition when they should be making use of highly competent professional assistants, oriented toward research, who can dig out of the morass of information available the relevant facts which would enable the making of more accurate and more discerning decisions. It is time to bring all the

---

20 Paul N. Elbin, "College President on a Tightrope," *College and University Business*, XXVIII, No. 4 (Oct., 1958), p. 21.

best research techniques into the process of administration. Experience and intuition, backed up appropriately by uncontestable facts, can make a much happier life in the academic community. The occupants of the ivy halls have long since left the cloistered retreats for the bustling marketplace. The skills and tools of this advanced age, placed at the service of a man with vision, courage, and character, can produce a college president who makes perceptive decisions.

It is quite probable that the time has come for the president of the college to garner his information from the wide variety of resources available to him and assume the same role in the academic community as his counterparts have already assumed in political life. Like the President of the United States and the Governors of the states, he should at the beginning of each year bring to the attention of the constituent members of the community the policy changes and innovations on which he would like their counsel. If he has properly analyzed educational needs and trends and tested the factors that relate to operational success, if he has conceived immediate and long range plans, and if he has had the benefit of the thinking of his most learned associates, then he does have a program to propose and even to defend. If the facts support his projects and projections, he has every expectation of winning a favorable response from his erudite colleagues.

No matter how many facts are considered and no matter how ably the faculty participates in recommending policy, the college president must not make the mistake of believing his job can be done for him. The field of decision-making has not been preëmpted; the president, for all the collaboration he may get, must bear the major decision-making responsibility himself.

He may expect that if the facts in a given situation are systematically collected, the conclusion will be quite obvious. He needs to acknowledge that the information-collecting stage can be unduly prolonged in an effort to avoid the unpleasantness of making a decision. He must be able to judge when it is premature to make a decision and he must know when such a judgment is procrastination. He must be aware of the influence of his moods on the choices he makes, and if his psychological variations necessitate, he should make decisions only when he is free of emotional encumbrance.

Sometimes the choice of alternatives will leave the administrator with a feeling of having lost as much as he gained. The happiest situations are those where a "yes" or "no" is the perfect answer, but such situations are rare. Inevitably, once the alternative courses of action are clear, the president must have the courage to select one. He then needs the fortitude and finesse to carry it through to a salutary conclusion.

CHAPTER IV

The Continuum

Alma Mater

The day-to-day activities of the college president—the pressing tasks that confront him and the manifold relations he experiences in dealing with students, faculty, fellow-administrators, and community leaders—may lead observers to make too close an identification of the institution with its chief administrator. It is wise for the college president, at least, not to make any such self-identification. The wisdom of such caution is doubly founded. It makes the burdens of his office more endurable and redounds to the ultimate benefit of the college. Although the historian's view in temporal perspective may not always commend itself to the impatient, it is the soundest view for both understanding and planning.

The president should accordingly be sensitive to the historical tenets of the college. Although change occurs, it is most often through slow evolution rather than through sudden mutation. What appears to be innovation may frequently be the repetition of an earlier, unsuccessful experiment. Colleges are disposed to mature gracefully and their best progress comes from gradual improvements experientially derived.

The president must realize that in a sense alma mater lives a life independent from that of any of her constituents. As an institution she does not merely mirror her successive presidents. Rather, she accepts this procession of honored leaders, realizing full well that she has a personality of her own. The college has a self-perpetuating momentum. A president may accelerate, decelerate, or veer her in her course, but destroy her impetus he cannot.

Of some relevance to this thought is an unpublished statement on the selection of a president for the University of California prepared by an Academic Senate Advisory Committee composed of faculty members from all campuses of the University.

In discussing the qualifications of the president for the function of shaping policy, the committee suggested that:

... he should be aware that the policy of a great university is the product of many minds: leadership he can give, and high purposes of his own creation are important; but he should be alert to the thoughtful suggestions of his faculty and other associates and seek the utmost use of their ideas.

He should bear in mind that two chief groups with which he deals—regents and faculty—are perpetual bodies: whatever the turnover of the individual members, each group has a perpetual tenure. For each group, policy questions have a background with origins antedating his administration and a prospect reaching beyond his tenure of office. The group has its own direction and momentum: he cannot change them drastically, but he can secure moderate diversion in the course and moderate alterations in the pace, if he can persuade the group that his purposes are wise.[1]

Presidential Vision and Imagination

The many facets of the college, the many forces that shape its destiny, the many variations in thought of the people who make up its constituent members give a college a distinct personality. As Dr. Robert M. Hutchins declared in his discussion of the administrator, a primary responsibility of the president is to discover the aims and ends of the college he comes to lead.[2] Once in tune with his institution, he must have the vision and the imagination to help shape its destiny. Its independent personality will respond to his inspiration. Its impressionableness will yield to his leadership—especially so if his efforts are directed toward keeping his college in pace with the change in the social order.

Expectations of the College by Society

The American society's view of its colleges has reflected current values. In early days when institutions of higher learning were the source of spiritual and lay leaders, such institutions were held in high regard. Under the impact of Jacksonian democracy and in a nation where culture and social adornments were frowned upon, nineteenth century collegiate institutions were in many cases threatened with extinction if they failed to open their doors to less socially

---

[1] "Tentative Thoughts . . . ," by Acad. Senate Committee.
[2] Hutchins, *op. cit.,* p. 404.

favored students and their curricula to courses of practical application.

As the continent has been subdued to the machine, there has been a growing concern for and interest in the proper use of leisure.

Today in many communities colleges and universities serve as cultural centers. As commercialism invades the theater and other forms of entertainment, institutions of higher learning are providing livelihoods for authors and composers and other artists whom they bring to their faculties, and opportunities for creative experiences for their students.

America seems to view its colleges and universities with a double image. On the one hand, education is conceded to be valuable, but the value is measured in terms of the college graduate's earning power. On the other, there is a current of anti-intellectualism that sweeps into a sea of ridicule "long-haired" tastes or theories.

What should be the president's role where there is such conflict in values? Here is an opportunity for him to exercise the best of leadership. Certainly he renders higher education a disservice by perpetuating the dollar value upon it. It is incumbent upon him to assert those values which express the highest goals of higher education, the search for truth and the right of free inquiry.

At the same time he cannot ignore the needs and concerns of the community his institution serves, but he must assess these within the goals and aims of the college. To the community he must make explicit the role of the college, and to his faculty he must interpret community interests and concerns. At times he may be merely a mediator, but often he will exert leadership influence.

The college is, or should be, a place of intellectual ferment. Alma mater encourages stimulation of creativity. She fosters ideation and exchange of information. She is a center for painstaking thought, a haven for reflection and deliberation. The president may well be the source of inspiration and encouragement for the unending search for knowledge and truth.

The public expects the college to maintain a high quality in the educational program for all students. Professional educators are aware of this need, and all concerned have shared their views through professional and popular publications. Those involved in this issue hold varying views on the relative merits of so-called aca-

dent sets a pattern to follow. These factors are not defined as specifically as they once were but the college president, among the many qualities which the public associates with his office, is expected to be a "good" man in the moral sense.

A high level of conduct is also expected of the administrative and teaching faculty, and members of the board of control. The moral tenets may not be so directly applied to the individuals but as deliberative bodies charged with the mission of determining policy for the college, the same responsibility applies.

> The trust function of trustees, and it is a critical and difficult one, is to stand firmly as lay interpreters and defenders of the college or university's high purposes and function in the larger civic community; to see and protect the differences between long-range public service and short-range public . . . servility.[4]

The quest of the college is truth. High-mindedness in every relationship characterizes the search; that which does not qualify is discarded. The college can and does get involved in tangential missions; inevitably it extricates itself and pushes ahead on the major course: the discovery and revelation of truth.

A young colleague in his commencement address declared, the college is a place where there is emphasized: "an atmosphere of free inquiry, free discussion and controversy; an atmosphere of hard work and individual stress, and an atmosphere of sensitivity to values."

The American college is not expected to provide a leveling experience. Under no circumstances is its aim related to suppression, but rather to the cultivation of natural diversity. It is concerned with equality in the American sense—equality not as the end but as a beginning, as the provision of opportunity to explore and develop the innate talents and abilities of the society. The whole idea is one of growth, growth in attainment of knowledge and growth in the insights that make the attainment of knowledge meaningful. Harold Taylor said:

> It is fairly easy to convey information to students, and if this were all that higher education had to do, it could operate most effectively through television, correspondence courses, simple textbooks, and mass lectures. In the matter of values, however, it is the day

---

[4] James Lewis Morrill, *The Ongoing State University* (Minneapolis, Minn.: University of Minnesota Press, 1960), p. 46.

to day life of a university community, where students and teachers talk and work together, and where their personal relationships involve them in the common educational purpose, that students learn to make discrimination between truth and falsehood, good argument and bad, good style and rhetoric, and where they learn to develop their own intellectual character. The ideal university is one in which there is general recognition among students and faculty alike that the work they are doing together is a significant part of the development of their own civilization.[5]

It is especially in the wider realm of ideas that alma mater perpetuates herself. Organizational procedures, monetary needs, public relations issues, the influence of segments of the constituency of the college, the impact of individual personalities are as relevant to the life course of alma mater as the changing of the guard is to the security of the state.

The main stream of ideas may dwindle to a trickle in times of intellectual drought. In other times and other seasons that stream may rage and swell and overflow the banks of complacency and inertia.

------

[5] Taylor. *op. cit.*, p. 82.

A college's most recent experience can be a very important determinant as to the qualifications desired in its president. Alma mater may be a timeless, continuing entity, but she can suffer from too much of the same thing. If the college has been short of funds and is in desperate straits, a successful fund raiser is needed. Other factors will always be important, but in a period of impecuniousness it is necessary to have a president who can bring in material resources. If there has been a series of unsettling changes under the previous administration, a campus may need an administrator who can consolidate and fortify the gains made rather than continue an aggressive program of development. For the institution that has a great deal of conflict and controversy, a peacemaker is required.

An institution may experience cycles with alternating periods of rapid and startling change and periods of relative calm. The impact of the personality of the president, and his range and variety of talents, may be a most influential factor in the life of the college. Sound presidential timber includes both the flamboyant extrovert and the sheltered scholar. For a time a college will prosper under a dynamic, hard-driving attention-getter, who endeavors to take an active part in every facet of the institution's life. He is a stirrer-upper, an abolisher of football teams, or a proponent of national championships. If he wants Pulitzer Prize winners on his faculty, he gets them, and he may even get Nobel laureates. He persuades philanthropic foundations to invest large sums of money in projects on his campus. After experience with such an aggressive leader, the board of trustees may turn to the quiet, productive scholar. To be sure of relief, they may even unwittingly choose a man who would qualify as the Office-holder of Robert M. Hutchins.[2] The college may operate quite happily under the aegis of such a president. When both apathy and unrest develop, a need for more innovation in its academic life becomes apparent and another cycle may well begin.

The list of presidential qualifications is quite varied because of the many kinds of colleges which are now part of higher education in the United States. The junior college, the municipal college or university, the state college, the large state university—all have their individual needs. So too have the private universities, the private liberal arts colleges, and the church-related institutions. In view of

---

[2] Hutchins, *op. cit.*, pp. 397-98.

this diversity, it is unlikely that presidential qualifications will ever fall within a limited pattern. If collegiate institutions were devoted simply to excellence in teaching and the search for truth, presidents who could lead the institutions toward these two goals might have many similar qualifications. But the great range of interests, aims, states of growth and development, and cultural orientations, as well as the differences in geographical location among American colleges, are reflected in the wide span of qualities required and represented in their presidents.

Analysis of Personal and Professional Qualifications

Felix C. Robb, one time dean of instruction at George Peabody College and later its president, has offered several pieces of advice to the new college president which serve well to point up criteria an experienced academic man feels are necessary for the presidency.[3] Aggressiveness and lack of timidity are among the requisites because the president seldom enjoys job tenure and yet he must act as though he did. He cannot, for example, yield to every request for public appearances; he depreciates their value if he makes a great many speeches. The president also must be a person able to work easily and selflessly with his colleagues. The college head ought not be a man over-sensitive to tensions and antagonisms. Dr. Robb believes real issues will generate friction on occasion but that such friction is preferable to a state of torpor. Certainly not the least of the requirements are intellectual ability, integrity, and involvement. If the institution's leader is to be respected by the faculty, he must know the interests and the motivations of a teaching staff.

A most discerning and complete statement on the personal and professional qualifications desired for a university presidential office was prepared by an Academic Senate Advisory Committee on the Selection of a President for the University of California.[4] The Committee assumed that the president of the University would be a man able to serve a statewide institution and at the same time work closely with its regents, the legislature, his administrative subordinates, the faculty, the students, the alumni, and the general public.

---

[3] Felix C. Robb, "An Open Letter to a New College President," *College and University Business* (Feb., 1962), pp. 35-8.
[4] "Tentative Thoughts . . . ," by Acad. Senate Committee.

ment.[7] He will be joined by his closest associates in administration and by the high-minded members of his faculty. Together they will continue the endless pursuit of the truth, which is the aim of all higher education.

Personal Qualities

In the process of charting the course of the college, the president needs not only prudence, courage, fortitude, and justice, so eloquently supported by Mr. Hutchins in his article *The Administrator*, but also the further quality of resilience. Almost every day of his professional life will be spent working with people and their problems. Frequently the problems are set forth in stormy sessions that tax severely his emotional restraint and stability. If he is to bounce back from a series of experiences of this kind, he must have cultivated the habit of resilience. In his office he wears a mantle of authority which defines in a way the nature and extent of his freedom. His freedom is realized in the pursuit of the end he envisions for the college which he heads. It is a freedom to make decisions in keeping with the vision, and this freedom he must maintain.

In the process of working toward realizing his conception of the college, he needs personal and social sensitivity, understanding, and a happy faculty of ego-building in his relationships with his colleagues on the administrative and teaching faculty.

When a member of the college staff is in acrimonious disagreement with the president and an exchange of personal feelings follows, a major responsibility rests on the president to encourage conciliation. The colleague, who has differed sharply with him, has a face-saving problem; the president has the institutional perspective. The president works continuously at maintaining an objective point of view. The position he holds and the role he plays require the surmounting of personal animosities.

One of the most puzzling problems confronting the executive is the way in which little things can "rob him of his bigness." Roy Pearson takes the concept from the *Song of Solomon* that it is the little foxes that spoil the vineyard.[8] The little foxes of Mr. Pearson

---

[7] Robert M. Hutchins, "The Administrator Reconsidered: University and Foundation," 1955, *Freedom, Education and the Fund, Essays and Addresses, 1946–1956* (New York: Meridian Books, 1956), pp. 187-89.

[8] Roy Pearson, "Little Sins that Ruin Big Men," *Think*, XXVII, No. 6 (June, 1961), pp. 17-18.

are jealousy, anger, fear, and greed, which can cause as much trouble as grand larceny. He suggests these are only a few of the little foxes that spoil the executive vineyards. But when a vineyard is destroyed, or a college seriously harmed, it makes little difference whether the despoiler was a big fox or a little one.

The office of the college presidency requires a great deal of self-discipline on the part of the incumbent. Among those who are selected for the responsibility of giving leadership to the college, the successful are those who enjoy a generous measure of self-restraint. For the release of emotional tension that is required, the president needs among his immediate subordinates one or more who are his "wailing walls." It is important that such subordinates be themselves people of high moral integrity, that their discretion be unquestionable.

The too-serious president is handicapped in his frequent brushes with associates on and off the campus. Perhaps only experience can teach him the proper time to make fun of his strained personal conflicts. There is a right and wrong time to laugh away the frictions. The important achievement is to laugh with the person in conflict or about the incident. It is almost never good strategy to laugh at the aggrieved.

Among the faculty on some campuses are accomplished administrator baiters. These people are usually articulate resisters of authority. They enjoy the role they play and often assume a responsibility of speaking for the faculty. They thrive on contradiction; they pride themselves on being the loyal opposition. Such persons may temporarily be leading spokesmen and they may have both tenure and prestige among their peers. Clashes with such abrasive people require a high degree of resiliency on the part of the president. But most of all the facility of rolling with the punches, we in the rough and tumble matches frequently staged in the academic arena will require a keen sense of humor on the part of the person who sits in the president's chair.

When all the other members of the college community are down-hearted, disappointed, and even pessimistically viewing a failure to realize a grand goal of the college, it is the president's responsibility to be optimistic, to take the sanguine view that bad days are followed by good ones. He is the builder of faith in the resistance of

as rare as "a diamond in a coal mine." [13] He must be a fund-raiser who will be effective even though he won't get credit for it. He must be able to understand a budget and utilize it as an educational instrument. He will need to serve as spokesman for the college; and, because the public expects it, he must act as spokesman for the faculty as well. He must be competent in the area of public relations. The sureness demanded in this area, Stoke declares, is such that the "president's mind must be an electronic calculator which can give him instantly some estimate of the effect of any event, proposal, comment, or utterance upon the faculty, students, alumni, legislators, donors, critics, and friends." [14] He needs to be a man who will try to understand the faculty's psychology. "He must learn to blend humility, generosity, sensitivity, and poise into workable relationships with his colleagues." [15] Like an actor, he must know how he appears to others.[16]

Stoke also finds that the college president needs a quality which he calls "philosophical resignation" to draw on when everything possible has been done. "What he cannot help he must accept." [17] Still another requirement is placed at the head of the list by Stoke: "The most important qualification a college president can bring to his job," he declares, "is a philosophy of education." He needs this to give his institution direction and "to serve him *every day* as a guide for administrative decisions. A college president without a philosophy of education is a pilot without navigation charts." [18]

Former president Wriston gives greatest emphasis to a highly important quality: "a commitment to higher education which no discouragement [can] shake—indeed, with which nothing [can] successfully compete." [19] He is also deeply convinced that the president ought to be a scholar, even though nonscholars have been very successful college presidents. Although it is not likely the president will teach, it is well that he come to his job equipped with teaching experience. Wriston also regards a doctorate from a good university

---

[13] Stoke, *op. cit.*, pp. 3, 54.
[14] *Ibid.*, p. 103.
[15] *Ibid.*, p. 29.
[16] *Ibid.*, pp. 56, 63, 94, 107, 116, 159.
[17] *Ibid.*, p. 160.
[18] *Ibid.*, p. 161.
[19] Wriston, *op. cit.*, p. 19.

and college administrative experience as proper elements in a president's preparation.[20]

Former president Hutchins has stated that the university administrator must have "courage, fortitude, justice, and prudence or practical wisdom." [21] The last virtue mentioned may be assumed to cover the more technical qualifications found in the able and experienced administrator. Hutchins at first specifically excluded the quality of patience, but subsequently he reversed himself on the ground that "the university president who wants *durable* action, not just action, must have patience, and have it in amounts equal to the durability desired." [22]

President Peter Sammartino, of Fairleigh Dickinson University, is being only partially humorous when he indicates that the president would do well to have a cast iron stomach because of the variety of food he is subjected to, and obviously is fully serious when he declares that "a college president needs above all a sense of humor." [23] The college head also ought to be a man who has friends outside the college and outside higher education. Regardless of the pressures of time he ought to be a man who maintains an interest in cultural activities such as music, theater, and literature, and sets an example for his faculty.[24]

President Donald Walker, of Idaho State College, made several valuable observations on presidential qualifications after he had been in office a year—a time at which the selection process could be viewed in light of the impact of the office. He felt that in addition to considering specifications based on job analyses, boards of trustees should give careful thought to certain fundamental factors in the candidates' personalities.

As Walker suggests, the college president needs to be flexible, as he will have to move rapidly and effectively. He practices the art of the possible; but he cannot be Machiavellian or overly expedient. He needs to be courageous, for he will have to bear criticism over long periods. The president who feels excessive need to please will dissipate his energy, become uncertain in his decision, and ultimately antagonize everyone. He must also be a man who can play

[20] *Ibid.*, pp. 16, 19, 28-9, 59.
[21] Hutchins, "The Administrator," p. 396.
[22] Hutchins, "The Administrator Reconsidered," p. 187.
[23] Sammartino, *op. cit.*, pp. 12, 16.
[24] *Ibid.*, pp. 14-15.

the role of president. He needs to be one who can maintain a calm, firm demeanor in the face of frenzied activity and contradictory counsel. He must be able to absorb the feeling of uncertainty which periodically develops in the faculty and other campus groups. His attitude must express optimism and confidence. The man chosen to be college president must be of sound character. "This may sound a bit old-fashioned, but I am convinced that the essence of good administration is integrity and character." He must have an impeccable personal life, an appealing public image, and must resist the temptation to self-aggrandizement. In addition, the president must be basically democratic. President Walker believes the position is not primarily one of command; it is, rather, one of leadership. A college community cannot be coerced or bullied over a long period of time; however, it does appreciate leadership.

It is Walker's opinion that future presidents will tend to be chosen from within higher education's own precincts:

> I predict, and it is only a prediction, that we may be entering a transitional period in which college presidents will be increasingly from college communities from among individuals with a background of administrative experience.[25]

Whatever their experience and however long their tenure in office, college presidents all seem to agree there is an enormous number of requirements for office and an extreme scarcity of men who can meet them. Wriston expresses this well when he writes:

> ... few men have all the talents—very few. Most have limited abilities. No one whom I have ever known could do all the things expected of a college president and do all of them well. Often a man is suited to part of the task, that part which is most urgent at the moment of his appointment.[26]

---

[25] Letter to the author from Dr. Walker.
[26] Wriston, *op. cit.*, p. 20.

CHAPTER VI

The Vista

Colleges have not played a consistent role in society. They have been in and out of the societal stream. The college or university has a detached view: it watches, as it were, the life of the community go by. If the college has actively entered the stream of the life of its community, it has inevitably assumed a major leadership role. Notable among the involved participants have been a number of well known Ivy League colleges that have assumed directional responsibilities of considerable magnitude.

This duality of participant and detached observer may continue; however, so much emphasis is now placed on college attendance, so much attention is focused on the college, so much research sponsored by industry is centered on campuses, that the role of the detached observer is less possible. The marketplace, not the ivy tower, appears to be the setting for the college of the future.

The primary concern of college laboratories and classrooms was once pure research. Scholars engaged in research for research's sake. The students explored problems to learn the techniques and the procedures of investigation. Now a great deal of the research on college campuses is applied research. It is subsidized by industries, by government, and by business for the purpose of improving a product or a technique or a sales program. The college president is confronted with contractual questions and is rightly concerned with the long-range impact of these associations. There may be a danger in this trend. The great occasional innovations that emerged when the object of research was less specific may be lost in the process of the applied research. On the other hand, this reliance on the college for the research which is essential to the progress of business and industrial life may mark a trend away from privately organized and subsidized research institutes which are unallied with colleges and universities. Furthermore it may bring about the partnership of higher education and business, which can have mutually beneficial influences.

Much attention has centered around the increasingly active leadership responsibilities assumed in political affairs by teaching and administrative faculty of colleges and universities. Many college teachers have become part-time consultants in industry, and civic, and cultural organizations. So prevalent, in fact, is this development that limitations on the extent of such extracurricular activities have been thought necessary by many boards of control. These activities point up the dynamism of the college; it is a place where changes can and do take place, where ferment and participation are not unwelcome. A new concept of service to society is sweeping the collegiate institutions into the stream of progress.

The maladjustments which are appearing in society, partially if not largely because of its progress, offer a great challenge to American colleges and their presidents. Automation in production and distribution of goods and services, with the threatening impact to occupational outlets and job security, poses problems for study and investigation to college presidents and other college leaders. It is quite probable that extension services as well as other agencies of adult education will continue to grow in importance as facets of higher education.

A further major societal consideration is focused on the increasing interest in college education. Once a small fraction of college-age youth were in college. Now in several states as many as half of these youths are in college. For the nation as a whole, if the trend of the past decade continues, 57 per cent of the college age population will be in college by 1978; and in some states between 70 and 80 per cent will be enrolled.[1] The magnitude of the range of individual differences which will thus be brought to college campuses has already caused grave concern. Efforts to change this trend will not be successful, although some students may be diverted to special kinds of colleges.

The rapid increase in the number of junior colleges indicates the very important role which this community-centered college will have in the next decade. This uniquely American institution began as the lower division of the traditional four-year college, and

---

[1] Ronald B. Thompson, *Enrollment Projections for Higher Education, 1961–1978* (Curtis Reed Plaza, Menasha, Wisc., American Association of Collegiate Registrars and Admissions Officers, Sept., 1961). Thompson presents tables of enrollment projections for the United States as a whole and for each of the fifty states.

changed to a multi-purpose institution during the depression of the 1930's. The junior college has a major responsibility for salvaging students with latent talents. A great number of potential collegians have abilities, sometimes undiscovered, that fall outside those most useful for traditional college entrance examinations. Many students who can do well in some phases of higher education may not do particularly well with the traditional liberal arts programs. It has long been known that young people with high mechanical and social abilities may do less well in handling abstract symbols. Yet these other abilities must be discovered and refined if the country is to maintain the pace of its technological progress.

> If ever there was a time when the individual could become the victim of a system, that time is almost upon us. The concern of high schools over "the class record for college entrance" and the concern of the college over the improvement of its "corporate image" are both disgraceful, in the light of what is beginning to happen to Jim and Jane and Bob and Betty.[2]

The temptation to regard individuals as dispensable grows as enrollments increase. Colleges too frequently take pride in the attrition rate instead of the retention record, and unless a genuine concern is felt for the individual student, these attitudes will prevail.

To cope with the variety and range of individual differences, higher education must provide great diversity in its institutions, a broad range of curricula, and accurate measurements of individual abilities and potentials. There should be a refinement of admissions standards and flexibility in admissions practices. The statement of admissions should be a most significant indication of the philosophy of the institution. Once the student is admitted, the institution should pride itself on his continued educational progress.

Many factors need to be considered in predicting success in college, including such elusive elements as motivation, drive, and attitude. These need to be the subjects of intense research and experimentation. President Eddy of Chatham College suggests indirectly some ideas that also need study: the general education plan, the orientation of the faculty, the nature and breadth of co-curricular activities, and the level of expectancy in academic work.[3]

---

[2] Edward D. Eddy, Jr. "We Should Be *More* Concerned About Our Students," *College and University Business,* XXX, No. 1 (July, 1961), p. 28.

[3] *Ibid.,* p. 28.

There is so much to be learned, and the professional life of a person is comparatively so short, that all the devices and services which may contribute to the educational process should be brought into use. Continued experimentation with television as a supplement to the classroom activity, further exploration and experimentation with mechanical learning devices that enable scholars to work individually, and wider experience with the whole concept of independent study provide possible means of meeting the educational needs of our students. The trimester plan aimed at extending the school year is receiving justified attention. The University of Pittsburgh, one of the institutions engaged in the accelerated program, is generously sharing its findings with sister institutions.[4]

It is quite probable that the techniques of teaching may change appreciably during the next two decades. The change in pattern of student interests and needs, and the higher ratio of students to qualified faculty, will inevitably affect the size and perhaps the shape as well as the nature of the classroom and the classroom activities.

Under the president's direction the college community must reassess the importance as well as the place of the physical plant in the learning process. The college needs to look critically at the ratio of regular to special rooms. Detailed planning will be essential if the full impact of multisensory aids on the learning process is realized. The experimentation with closed and open circuit television, the advent of and refinement in teaching machines, the research results in the area of behavioral science which bear upon the nature of the learning activity—all will influence the nature of the physical plant. It is too wasteful of money and time to permit resolution of these problems by trial and error.

Tremendous support must be given to institutional research in the colleges if the challenge of the future is to be met. As an observant educator has pointed out, higher education can profitably consider the experience of industry in respect to the benefits to be gained from research investment. In general, the businesses and in-

---

[4] The University of Pittsburgh periodically issues a *Progress Report on Year 'Round Education* which contains current information on the University's own program as well as that of other institutions with a similar calendar; see also Edward H. Litchfield, "Tri-Mester: Education of Superior Quality in a Shorter Period of Time," *College and University Business*, XXXI, No. 1 (July, 1961), pp. 24-7. Views opposing the tri-mester plan may be found in the Summary Report on the Discussion Groups of the sixteenth national conference on higher education of the Association of Higher Education, Chicago, Ill., March 6-7, 1961.

dustries which make the greatest progress are those which spend the highest percentage of their funds on research and development. In the chemical industries, which have grown with marked success since World War II, 3–5 per cent of gross sales were spent on research. In sharp contrast, education has been spending less than one tenth of one per cent of its expenditures on research.[5]

If the proper development of the college is to take place, the long-range planning effort will need more careful attention than it has had at any time in the past. It will be essential for each college to have a high ranking officer with sufficient staff to gather, collate, interpret, and project the statistical data bearing on administrative decisions.

All the facets of the institution should be represented on a committee to advise the administrative officer in charge of the research service. A primary responsibility of the advisory committee should be the dissemination of information to the members of the college community about the factors that bear upon the development and growth of the college. The advisory committee should keep the planning officer informed of the interests, needs, and even the anxieties of the faculty, the students, and the patrons of the institution.

Planning decisions should be based primarily on factual information. Appropriately, all this information will have a major influence on the planning and development of the facilities of the college.

The interrelationship of college management responsibilities is increasingly evident. Staffing, teaching, construction, purchase of equipment, and changes in the general character of students all relate not only to capital outlay but to every other component of the institution. The president's leadership responsibility is as varied as the services of the campus. He supervises the preparation and control of the budget, and the expenditure of the funds, and his efforts must be of the same gigantic proportions in raising the required funds.

Fund raising, always an important responsibility of the president, will be increasingly significant in the years ahead. An indication can be derived from the experience of the immediate past. From 1948 to 1958 California increased its capital expenditures for pub-

---

[5] Philip H. Coombs, "The Greatest Shortage in Education," *The Clearing House*, XXXV, No. 4 (Dec., 1960), pp. 195-200.

licly supported colleges and universities by 581 per cent.[6] During the same decade the private colleges and universities of California increased their capital expenditures by 210 per cent. During this same period, current operating expenses for the state colleges of California increased 345 per cent while the same expenditures for the University of California increased by 174 per cent. The current operating expenses for the private colleges and universities in California increased 94 per cent during this ten-year period.[7]

In New York State there were 205,000 full-time and 196,000 part-time students in the public and private collegiate institutions in 1959. By 1980 that state expects the number of students in both categories will be considerably more than doubled with 551,000 enrolled full-time and the same number part-time.[8] A study in Florida showed that state has every expectation of exceeding its 1955 enrollment of 44,526 collegians with a 1970 level of approximately 132,000—an increase of nearly 200 per cent.[9]

In 1958 undergraduate full-time enrollment in the University of California and the State Colleges of California was 87,629 students. It is estimated that the enrollment in the state colleges and the University of California will be 180,650 in 1975. This projected figure anticipates diverting a very large number of lower division students who would normally go to the University and the State Colleges to the junior colleges of that state.

Since these experiences probably will be typical, it is reasonable to assume that the presidents of the publicly supported colleges throughout the United States will be spending a great deal of their energies making clear to the state legislatures that higher education needs additional funds. If the responsibilities to young people are

---

[6] This figure excludes the junior colleges, since no state appropriations have been made for capital outlay for these institutions.

[7] Technical Committee on the Costs of Higher Education in California, *The Costs of Higher Education in California, 1960–1975,* a report prepared for the Master Plan Survey Team and the Liaison Committee of the Regents of the University of California and the State Board of Education (Berkeley and Sacramento, Calif.: The Committee, 1960).

[8] *Meeting the Increasing Demand for Higher Education in New York State, A Report to the Governor and the Board of Regents,* Committee on Higher Education, Henry T. Heald, chairman (Albany, N. Y.: Board of Regents, State Education Department, Nov., 1960), pp. 54-55.

[9] A. J. Brumbaugh and Myron R. Blee, *Higher Education and Florida's Future, Recommendations and General Staff Report,* Vol. 1, (Gainesville, Fla.: University of Florida Press, 1956), pp. 28-29.

to be met, a larger percentage of the tax dollar will have to be spent on education. The same heightened efforts for fund raising will be required of the presidents of the private institutions. Colleges in the Ivy League, the Middle West, and the Far West have announced enormously ambitious plans to get more money in the immediate future. Through the efforts of such agencies as the Council for Financial Aid to Education, Inc., the public is becoming increasingly aware of the need and the efforts that will be required.[10]

Big business is diverting more of its resources to higher education, and small business is organizing itself to make a maximum contribution in this total effort. The time of the president of the college, already tightly scheduled, will have even more demands on it if the long-range planning function is to be properly managed. The president must realize that he more than any other person bears responsibility for charting the course and the progress of the college. At the same time the day to day unfolding of the long-range plan will require his expert leadership and direction.

The president will need to tap all the resources of the community he serves if he is to make the most advantageous decisions. It is suggested that he meet periodically with groups drawn informally from a cross section of his own faculty, students, parents, and patrons of the institution. These meetings can be brainstorming sessions, devoted to presenting information on the needs of the college as well as to encouraging the faculty, patrons, and the students of the college to present their dreams and hopes. Formal organizations are probably already sufficiently plentiful to keep the president informed through regular channels. Informal channels will permit him to check on popular opinion so that he can more successfully meet the demands of his leadership role.

Society's expectations of colleges and universities suggest special attention to the qualities and preparation of the person who is to serve as president. The placing of more and larger research contracts by business, industry, and foundations on college campuses requires that the president have a greater knowledge of law, taxation, and contractual procedures than has been necessary in the past. The increasingly competitive market for the highest levels of talent and educational achievement, and the knack of retaining this talent

---

[10] Council for Financial Aid to Education, Inc., 6 East 45th Street, New York, N. Y.

once engaged, require the president to have much more insight and ability in the area of personnel relations. The increasingly critical attitude toward the college community and the teaching for which it is responsible requires the president to have an intimate knowledge of the teaching process from firsthand experience and from periodic evaluations. The need to inform the public of the aims of the college and the success with which it is achieving them makes the public relations function more important than it has been in other decades. The management ability that is required to match a burgeoning enrollment with resources in materiel and personnel that have not been available in the same ratios will place increasing demands on the abilities and skills and the time of the president.

The trend in college administration is perceptible. The college president is the leader of a specialized team. He is the coordinator, the catalyst, the generalist who draws resource information from people especially prepared in special areas of college administration.

The college of the future will be more accessible and open to inspection. The increased research grants, the growing interest and participation of the public in the support and management of the college, and the booming enrollments are among the factors that are pushing the college into the center of the societal stream.

Change, which has become a part of modern life, requires a facility for adjustment which may make new demands on higher education. The restless pushing and drive which has characterized America has seemed to aim at the realization of a goal of security and serenity. People are impatient and irritated when national or international events interrupt their relentless drive toward these perhaps unattainable goals. Now it may be that there shall have to be less concern about security; perhaps serenity can come more readily if the probability is accepted that life itself is a continuous state of adjustment. If this assumption has merit, then it might imply that the organization and administration of the college needs the same kind of orientation. It has been suggested that a principal responsibility of the president is to discover and interpret the aims of his campus, and yet those aims must themselves change and adjust. In the management process organization charts have been developed showing relationships between echelons of authority and responsibility. These can become devices for stratifying and sterilizing the very dynamic quality which higher education requires. Perhaps it may be advisable to reevaluate periodically the various administrative functions of the college to determine whether a new alignment of responsibilities and functions is in order. After all, the college is essentially a community, and people even in major roles have abilities which may serve the institution very well during one period of its growth, after which the needs of the college change and require a different kind of personality to carry on the new trend. It may be well therefore to expect that every administrator in a college and university, dealing particularly with the area of instruction and research, be prepared and experienced in teaching. He would have tenure and continuity of employment in the instructional responsibility, and perhaps each year his services to the college in his administrative role would be evaluated periodically and a judgment made whether he should continue in his administrative responsibility or make way for new leadership.[11]

To keep abreast of the recent developments in the college field the administrative faculty needs refresher education as much or even more so than do members of the teaching faculty. For college presidents, it would be well to consider annual or semi-annual workshops to exchange the most recent information pertaining to management of colleges and universities. One or more of the major foundations might undertake the responsibility, or at least the financing, of such a workshop. There is probably no more important need in higher education than properly informed leadership.

Emphasis has been given to the president's responsibility in evaluating the progress of the college. Paul H. Davis has prepared a measurement device by which college presidents may be rated or, better still, rate themselves.[12] His ten-point scale includes scores on character and integrity, knowledge and scholarship, leadership, planning, democracy, authority and responsibility, facts, recruitment of faculty, recruitment of staff and volunteers. Certainly the qualities of college presidents are of concern to many people and it is important to judge them as objectively as possible.

Centers of study of higher education offer promise in two respects. They are places or centers to which administrative personnel

---

[11] A suggestion by Mr. Wriston for flexibility has already been noted on pp. 56-57.

[12] Paul H. Davis, "The Measure of a College President," *Liberal Education,* XLVI, No. 3 (Oct., 1960), pp. 359-404.

go for needed information and experience with respect to recent developments in higher education. They are preparation centers, too, for prospective college administrators. None has undertaken specifically to groom men for presidencies, although persons who are well prepared for one administrative post may well step up to the top position at a later time.

The only activity exclusively concerned with college heads is the President's Institute, directed by Professor Robert W. Merry, which has been in operation since 1955.[13] About three dozen recently appointed presidents are selected each year. The new presidents attend a series of case discussions and speeches by prominent figures in the field. The wives of Institute members also participate and attend a parallel series of lectures and discussions designed to aid them in their responsibilities as presidents' wives. Sessions at the Institute, which last a week, are not an education for the presidency. They are rather a psychological preparation for office. New presidents seldom are fully aware of what their job will exact from them, and few if any are fully equipped for their extremely demanding task. The sessions of the Institute are quite valuable in that the members come to understand their problems are far from unique. Many of its members believe that although they do get ideas on how better to conduct their office, they benefit most from losing the sense of isolation which the office imposes.

The University of Michigan's Center for the Study of Higher Education also has an institute which holds annual sessions to study the problems of college administration. Sixty high ranking college officers, including presidents, attend for a period of one week. The activities of the Center do not include an institute exclusively for American college presidents, as does Harvard's Institute, although it does have a three-week seminar for foreign university heads.

Training and experiences which may lead to a presidency are encouraged by a few organizations. The Carnegie Corporation sponsors a limited program aimed at aiding the travel of younger men interested in educational administration. Part of the expectation behind the program is that some future presidents will be

---

13 This Institute, supported by the Carnegie Corporation, is an activity of the Institute for College and University Administrators under the directorship of Professor Merry. It is closely associated with Harvard University Graduate School of Business Education.

benefited because of their participation. President Stoke observes
that they are benefited at least by being exposed to those looking for
a new college chief executive.[14] There are a few fellowships granted
in the hope that administrators will be developed, but they are not
aimed at developing presidents exclusively. The Center at the University of Michigan is prominent in this field, offering fellowships
in college and university administration for post-doctoral study by
those who already have college teaching or administrative experience.

There are several agencies which engage in research on the problems of higher education. These programs are not designed to prepare men for a presidential post, but to aid presidents and other
administrators. Under the directorship of Earl J. McGrath, Columbia Teachers College maintains a research institute. The Center for
the Study of Higher Education at the University of California in
Berkeley has sponsored valuable work related to the college student. The Southern Regional Educational Board in Atlanta, an
interstate agency serving the South, conducts research on the needs
of Southern higher education and facilitates cooperation among
colleges and universities in its region. A great deal of its work is
devoted to surveying the needs of the future, but it also works to
develop solutions to administrative problems. The Center at the
University of Michigan, besides offering the Institutes and fellowships referred to above, also conducts research on the organization
and administration of higher educational institutions.

Certain consulting services are available for the president to call
on. Again, the Michigan Center is active in this area, as are the
Southern Regional Education Board and the Institute for the Study
of Higher Education at Teachers College. Certain specialized consultation agencies are also available to aid in the administration of
limited areas within the president's responsibilities and peculiar to
higher education. One of these is provided by the National Federation of College and University Business Officers. In the fund raising
department, the president can call on a number of profit-making
companies which specialize in soliciting the constituencies of colleges and universities.

---

14 Stoke, *op. cit.*, p. 14, n. 4.

Higher education (*Cont.*)
  research, 8, 96
  responsibility for character develop-
    ment in early periods, 9
  students, 43-44
    discipline, 13
    gentlemen's agreement, 13
  teaching in early periods, 11
Hiram College, 15
Hopkins, Mark, 13
Horn, Francis, on faculty participation
  in administration, 71-72
Hughes, Raymond, 17
Hutchins, Robert M., "The Adminis-
    trator," 87-88
  on administration, 87-88
  on office-holders, 84
  on presidential responsibility, 76
  on qualifications for presidency, 93
Hyde, William DeWitt, 26

I

Idaho:
  Idaho State College, 93
Illinois, 30
Individual differences, 97
Industrial research expenditure, 98-99
Institute for College and University Ad-
  ministrators, 104 n
Institute for the Study of Higher Edu-
  cation (Columbia Teachers Col-
  lege), 105
Institutional research, 72-73, 87, 98-99
Ivy League, 95, 101

J

Jefferson, Thomas, 17
Johns Hopkins University, 14, 26
Jordan, David Starr, 16, 18
Junior colleges, 15, 22, 84, 96-97

K

Kansas, University of, 5
Kent, R. A., 46

L

Leadership, 19, 87
Lee, Robert E., 16, 22
Legal status of presidents, 30-31
Leverett, John, 6
Liberal arts, 97
Liberal arts colleges, 84

Libraries, 51
Liquor, rules governing use of, 9
Low, President, 14
Lowell, A. Lawrence, 15, 18
  on qualifications for presidency, 91

M

Mann, Horace, 21
Mather, Cotton, 21
Mather, Increase, 1, 11
Mayer, Frederick, *Creative Universities,*
  19
McGrath, Earl James, 105
McVey, Frank, 17
Merry, Robert W., 19, 104
Michigan, University of, 13, 22, 26, 91
Milliken, Robert A., 22
Mississippi, University of, 9
Morgan, Arthur E., 26
Morrill, James Lewis, *Ongoing State
  University,* 18
  qualifications for presidency of, 82-85

N

National Education Association, 15
National Federation of College and
  University Business Officers, 105
New York, higher education enroll-
  ments, 100
New York University, use of term *chan-
  cellor,* 5
Nott, Eliphilet, 12-13

O

Oxford University, 4

P

Paris, University of, use of title *rector,*
  5
Patience, 91
Pearson, Roy, on minor failings, 88-89
Pennsylvania, University of, 26
  early presidents not on board, 10-11
Philosophy of education, 78-79, 92
Pittsburgh, University of, 5, 98
Political activities, denied college pres-
  idents, 14
Power struggle, 70
Presidential messages, 51
Presidents' Institute, 104
Princeton University, selection of presi-
  dent, 32

Private colleges, requirements for presidency, 83-84
Provost, 6
  background of term, 6
  use of term, 6
Public relations, 44-48
  trustees' responsibility for, 61

Q

Queens College, 91

R

Recreation, 90
Rector, 5
  background of term, 5
  powers of office, 5
    Germany, 5
    Scotland, 5
  use of term, 4-5
Reed College, 26
Research grants, 95, 102
Retention policy, 78
Rhode Island, University of, 71-72
Robb, Felix C., on presidential qualifications, 85
Rockefeller, John D., 26
Roman law, 5

S

Sacco-Vanzetti case, 15
Sammartino, Peter, *The President of the Small College,* 18
  on observing teaching, 40
  on qualifications for presidency, 93
Sarah Lawrence College, 69-70
Savelle, Max, on faculty participation in decisions, 71
Schmidt, George, on clergy in the presidency, 6-7
Schools, improvement by college presidents, 15
Southern Regional Education Board, 105
Sproul, Robert Gordon, on qualifications for presidency, 90-91
Stanford University, 5
Stassen, Harold, 14
State colleges, 84
  qualifications for presidency of, 84
State universities, establishment of, 14
Stephens, Richard W., 35
Stoke, Anson Phelps, 50
Stoke, Harold, 17, 105

Stoke, Harold, (*Cont.*)
  on exercise of power, 22
  on president representing higher education, 23
  on qualifications for presidency, 91
  on scope of presidency, 3
Students, 23
  natural diversity of, 80
  salvage of, 78, 97
  with special gifts, 79
Swarthmore College, 3, 26
Syracuse University, use of term *chancellor,* 5

T

Tappan, Henry Philip, 13, 22
Taylor, Harold:
  on presidential leadership, 69-70
  on values, 80
Teaching, evaluation of, 40
Teaching faculty (*see also* Faculty):
  autonomy of, 4
  balance of viewpoint, 42
  discharge of members, 40, 41
  loyalties, 68-69
  participation in administration, 11, 12, 13, 50, 70-72
  policy-recommending function, 62
  promotion procedure, 41, 42
  recruitment of, 8, 38
  retention and promotion policy, 40, 41, 42
  representative body of, 11, 64
Teaching machines, 98
Tead, Ordway, 19
  on faculty participation in administration, 71
  on faculty philosophies, 42
Television instruction, 98
Tenure, 11, 30-31
Thwing, Charles F., *College Administration* and *College President,* 17
Toledo, University of, selection of president, 32
Tri-mester plan, 98 n
Truth, 80

U

Union College, 12, 13
Universities, 84

V

Van Hise, Charles, 15

Virginia, University of, 17
  selection of president, 32
Voltaire, 28

W

Walker, Donald, on qualifications for
  presidency, 93
Washington and Lee University, 16, 22
Washington, University of, 71
Wayland, Francis, 13
Western Reserve Eclectic Institute (Hi-
  ram College), 15
West Liberty State College, 72
Wheeler, Benjamin Ide, 26
White, Andrew Dickson, on qualifica-
  tions for presidency, 91
Who's Who in America, 21, 21 n
Willard, Joseph, address to students, 9
William and Mary, College of, 3 n
  use of term *chancellor,* 5
  control in early period, 5
  use of term *rector,* 5
  rules governing liquor, 9

Williams College, 13
Wilson, Woodrow, 15-16, 91
Wisconsin, University of, 15
Woodburne, Lloyd, *Principles of College and University Administration,* 19
Wriston, Henry M., 17, 32
  on administrative organization, 56
  on observing teaching, 40
  on presidential leadership, 51
  on qualifications for presidency, 86,
    94
  on scholarship and administration, 69
  on training for presidency, 82
  on trustees, 62

Y

Yale University, 26, 35
  discipline problems, 10
  early president not on board, 11
  under Jeremiah Day, 11
  use of title *rector,* 4